While I Still Can . . .

While I Still Can . . .

Rick Phelps

Library of Congress Control Number: 2012905335
ISBN: Hardcover   978-1-4691-8848-5
               Softcover   978-1-4691-8847-8
               Ebook   978-1-4691-8849-2
               Audio Book   978-1-4691-9285-7

This book was printed in the United States of America.

To order additional copies of this book, contact:
Xlibris Corporation
1-888-795-4274
www.Xlibris.com
Orders@Xlibris.com
110160

Acknowledgments

First and foremost I need to thank God. My struggle with this disease has brought me to a closer relationship with Him. I talk with Him every day. The tribulations that come with this disease have made it difficult for me to attend church because of the crowds and confusion, but a pastor of mine once said, "This may be God's house, but you don't have to be here to talk with Him."

I also need to thank everyone in my family who has supported me with love and has given me strength. I love you all.

My new family of Memory People, which has become such a special part of my everyday life.

Greg and Sue Randles who have been our closest friends for so many years and always will be.

Harry Urban for working on the cover designs and Joely Young for her photography work.

The doctors who have looked after my well-being.

Gary Joseph LeBlanc who took on the project of writing this book that has helped me fulfill one of my sincerest dreams.

And I especially need to thank the love of my life, Phyllis June. I've loved her since the first time I laid eyes on her back in 1977, and always will. She has stood by my side through the many challenges we've faced. I wouldn't be the man I am without her.

Rick Phelps

Contents

The disease softly ripples through our days. And then a wave! A large, long rolling wave. That overwhelms and consumes. We cannot predict when it will come. We cannot control it when it arrives. If we don't conform to the wants of these waves and follow their flows, they will break us. We conform and do what we need to remain whole. We're washed ashore, we stand upright. Walk and bend retrieving shells and pebbles from the sand. Shells of wisdom, pebbles of strength. Left behind by those who've been here before us. Memory People who feel what we feel. Memory People who share our thoughts. Memory People who know our hearts, Softly ripple through our days.

Written by Memory People member Renee Dowling

Introduction

I'm just a regular guy. I should say, I was just a regular guy. In the last few years things have changed dramatically in my life. This is the story of those changes.

Early Onset Alzheimer's Disease (EOAD) came into my life officially on June 30, 2010. That day changed everything. I knew I had a memory deficit for at least five years before my diagnosis, but getting people to listen, understand, hear me . . . well, that was my first hurdle.

I learned very quickly the meaning of the word "denial." Denial is huge with EOAD. Family, friends, coworkers, and even doctors can't seem to say the word "Alzheimer's."

In my case I assume it was because of my age. I was fifty-seven when I was diagnosed. Very young you say? Through research, and educating myself, I discovered that there are even people in their thirties who have some form of dementia.

You see, Alzheimer's is but one of the many brain disorders under the "umbrella" of dementia. It is indeed the most common, but again, there are many.

Extremely early in this journey, I felt compelled to tell

my story. I soon found out that it is not only my story, it's the story of hundreds of thousands of people struck by this horrible disease.

The tale is in my head. But how to get it on paper, that was my problem. After starting Memory People™, a social networking site on Facebook for patients, family members, caregivers, and advocates, I was constantly looking for "that" person, that one person who understood what Alzheimer's is and could help me with my mission.

Then the day came; Gary Joseph LeBlanc joined Memory People. Gary is a renowned author in the world of Alzheimer's. I soon found that out. I knew in my heart of hearts he was the man to help me tell my story.

Gary's latest book *Staying Afloat in a Sea of Forgetfulness* had just been released. He was busy promoting it, and when I asked him to collaborate with me on my book he told me perhaps after the first of the year.

What? Maybe I was wrong. Here we have a man who cared for his father for over ten years, managing to keep him at home! He had been there for him 24/7. He was the "caregiver's caregiver." And he's telling me, "Maybe after the first of the year"?

I didn't know Gary except from emailing him, and even though I was stunned, I understood "The World" doesn't stop because I have EOAD. I thanked him but told him that after the first of the year was just not doable.

You see, with EOAD, time itself is my enemy. I don't know if I have six months or six years to tell my story. I simply had to find another writer. And I would. But thank God, three days later, my phone rang. With EOAD, a ringing phone can be a major problem, but when I saw it was from Gary, I had to answer it. He began to tell me he had been thinking about all of this and had decided he could start on the book sooner. He had some loose ends on some things to tie up, but if I could agree to the date, he would indeed help me write the book.

That day changed my life, again. We, or I, didn't know how this would go. In the following pages you will take a journey—a journey like no other . . . a journey into the mind of an actual Alzheimer's patient.

Come with Gary and me, as we walk you through what this terrible disease does to the afflicted person, his family, friends, coworkers, and even his faith. You will not regret the time it takes to read this book. After reading it, please talk about it to as many people as you can. You, dear reader, can be of great value in spreading much needed awareness and also invalidate the many myths surrounding this frightening disease. Please help, as Gary and I have done, to change lives, one person at a time.

Rick Phelps

Chapter 1

Seventeen Minutes

It has been said that the course of one's life can change in a matter of minutes. I'm about to tell you the story of a man and his beloved family whose lives were turned upside down one summer morning, altering their paths forever.

Rick Phelps and his wife, Phyllis June, were driving the eighty minutes from their home in northeastern Ohio to Zanesville, for a first time appointment with a neurologist. After locating the office building and parking the car, they went in and introduced themselves to the receptionist. As a new patient, there were the standard forms to fill out attached to a well-weathered clipboard, so Rick sat down and filled in his name and address. Nothing seemed amiss until he came to the question of his date of birth; at this he drew a complete blank! Seeing he was struggling, Phyllis June, due to experience, took over completing the rest of the information and handed it back to the woman behind the counter.

It became obvious that Rick was growing increasingly uneasy. His hands were fidgety, and his eyes were shifting nervously to and fro, examining everything in the room from the deep blue carpet to how the furniture was coordinated to match the floor and the earth-toned cream-colored walls.

As he continued to look around, he found himself wondering what medical condition the other people in the waiting room were enduring. It astonished him that they didn't seem to have a care in the world. "How could they be in a neurologist's office and not seemed to be worried?"

Finally, Rick was called into a small examination room. He got up onto the butcher-papered examination table while Phyllis June sat in a chair close to him. Their ears were alert to any slight noise, hoping to hear the turn of the doorknob. Waiting for what felt like an eternity, at long last a tall graying man in his sixties entered the room and introduced himself as the neurologist.

Having already worked out everything he was going to say about the history of what he had been experiencing, Rick was about to open his mouth, but he never got a chance to utter a single word.

The doctor immediately dominated the conversation, informing the two of them that he had received all the results from the tests that the general practitioner had ordered, and he saw no reason for Rick to take any of them over again. Instead, what the doctor wanted to do was give Rick his own mini-mental exam in order to check his cognition. He asked Rick to count backward from one hundred, which he failed. Next he asked him to draw the face of a clock, making the hands read 11:15; he failed once again. Finally, he told Rick a short story, asking him to tap his leg every time he heard the word "I." This too was a failure.

Putting his paperwork down, the doctor looked first at Phyllis June and then, more intently, at Rick. He said without hesitation, "I'm certain you have MCI/EOAD." Confused, Rick straight out asked, "What the heck is that?" The doctor explained, "It's mild cognitive impairment of early-onset Alzheimer's disease. I'm going to prescribe a newer medication called Exelon which comes in a patch. Change it every twenty-four hours and I'll see you in six months."

That was that. So within seventeen minutes of entering the building, Rick Phelps and his wife, Phyllis June, found out that, at age fifty-seven, Rick had Alzheimer's, a fatal disease!

They soon learned that Alzheimer's is the fifth leading cause of death in the United States.

Their lives would never be the same.

"Hope is a good thing, maybe the best of things, and no good thing ever dies."

—Unknown Author

Submitted by Memory People member Kathy Turner Montgomery

Chapter 2

Doctors!

As far back as 2005, Phyllis June began noticing that Rick was making uncommon mistakes, and for every mistake he made he cleverly fabricated an excuse. She found herself becoming a bit annoyed with him, believing it was just "typical male behavior." It seemed to her that he would only remember things that were important to *him*. Even on shopping trips with a grocery list in hand, he would only return home with half the items, mostly things that *he* favored.

Later, in 2007, Rick opted to take a class so that his status at work could be upgraded to Intermediate EMT, allowing him to be able to deal with administering certain medicines and handle other more advanced procedures. He would come home from the class frustrated, telling his wife "I just don't get it. The instructor only reads to us from a book. There's no actual training." Unfortunately, Rick failed the exam. At the time, Phyllis June truly believed it was because he hadn't studied hard enough, so she encouraged him to take the test over again. Rick simply refused. He knew in his heart he wouldn't be able to pass it, even a second time.

When Rick's symptoms first surfaced back in 2003, he spoke with his local family doctor, explaining that he was having problems with his memory. The doctor felt that this was most likely a result of depression from the grief of the sudden death of his daughter Jody.

At the young age of twenty-two, Jody had been admitted to the hospital for a routine procedure. Deplorably, something went terribly wrong and, tragically, she was pronounced dead early the next morning.

One of the problems Rick had with his doctor's theory was that this had happened all the way back in 1997. Granted, he missed his daughter dearly, but he remained skeptical of this diagnosis. However, with the typical feeling of "your doctor knows best," he agreed to take the prescribed antidepression and antianxiety medications, and then he continued on with his everyday life, as he had been told.

Despite following his doctor's orders, taking various medications and attempting to get beyond whatever it was that was disturbing him, Rick's condition only worsened. Even though his symptoms increased, his doctor continued to show a great lack of concern. He continued to tell Rick that these symptoms were a direct result of nervousness, fatigue, and stress. Not knowing what else to think, Rick just kept doing what he was told.

Finally, after seven long, confusing years of being incorrectly diagnosed, his doctor performed a mini-mental exam on him. Rick scored poorly. The doctor was surprised and somewhat baffled with the test results, so he proceeded to order a blood test, checking to see if maybe he was vitamin B deficient. The findings were negative, so they moved on from there to a CAT Scan imaging of Rick's brain.

After all the years of being misunderstood and not being listened to, he was finally being sent to visit a neurologist.

Once I accepted my diagnosis of Early-Onset Alzheimer's, I decided to meet it the way I have met all difficulty in my life—with-a-spit-in-your-eye attitude and a sense of humor.

So I unofficially adopted the Cheshire Cat as my mascot. "All right," said the Cat; and this time it vanished quite slowly, beginning with the end of the tail, and the grin, which remained some time after the rest of it had gone.

So that's my "philosophy"; all right, Alzheimer's got me, but I plan on vanishing slowly and having my grin remain for a very long time.

Written by Memory People member Donnamarie Baker

Chapter 3

After the Diagnosis

The drive home from the neurologist's office felt like part of a nightmare—totally surreal. Slowly, reality began to set in. Could they really have just received the definitive diagnosis that Rick, an otherwise youthful fifty-seven-year-old, had Alzheimer's?

As he rolled this over in his mind, Rick found that there was a small sense of comfort in knowing that he had finally received an explanation about what had been happening to him for all those years. But on the other hand, Phyllis June interrupted his thoughts, declaring that this doctor must be out of his mind! "How can you have Alzheimer's? You're not even old!" She sighed and, glancing sympathetically over at her husband, she continued, "As soon as we get home, I'm calling our family doctor. This can't be right. You're only in your fifties."

The rest of the ride home consisted of "Hey, remember when I made the mistake of . . ." or "No wonder I couldn't remember how to get there . . ." This brought on a wave of guilt for Phyllis June. She began to realize how long she must have been in denial. She wondered to herself, "What if the doctor is right?" Finally, the conversation led to "What are we going to do?" and "What about your job?"

As they drove along, new questions began popping into their heads. Some they verbalized, others they kept to themselves. But one thought in particular began to bother Rick incessantly—this doctor had just told him "I'll see you in six months." After delivering such a devastating diagnosis, what kind of doctor could just leave it at that?

Early the following morning, Rick was on the phone to his neurologist. He informed the doctor, "I'm not thrilled with you just telling me to come back in six months. What am I supposed to do now?" The doctor simply instructed him to remain as stress-free as possible and continue on with his life as normally as he could. What? That seemed absurd! So Rick hung up the phone and just shook his head. "How the heck am I supposed to stay stress-free!"

Spending the remainder of the morning researching Alzheimer's on the Internet, he finally came across a local Alzheimer's organization which had a 24/7 helpline. As fast as he could he called the number, giving the woman on the other end of the phone a brief history of what had just transpired and how long it had taken to get there. She immediately set up an appointment for a counselor to come and visit them at home the following evening. Having been instructed that this should be a family meeting Phyllis June called their daughter Tia, explaining a little bit of what was going on. Tia and her husband, Brian, agreed to be there for the meeting but had a feeling of apprehension in their hearts.

The next evening, as promised, the counselor arrived

and the family invited her to sit at the kitchen table. She then proceeded to spend the next three hours educating these bewildered souls on the many aspects of this debilitating disease. Sitting around the table, they attempted to digest huge amounts of information about Alzheimer's and what the future may hold. During these hours they learned more from this kind woman than from any doctor or medical professional ever! Rick explained that he could remember what he and Phyllis June had done on a certain day, twenty-some-years ago, but he couldn't even tell you what he had for lunch earlier that afternoon! The counselor told them "one of the first things you all must realize is that Rick has already started to lose his memory backward. His short-term memory will go first and then eventually he will begin losing his long-term." She went on to say that they all, as a family, should spend as much time together as possible. "Rick, you have to start changing your life, starting today! Stress is out. It will only cause more complications for you and possibly cause the disease to advance more rapidly."

It was a truly amazing and yet disconcerting experience. Just three short hours prior not one of the family members in attendance had any idea what they were in for. Now they all had a new awareness of this thing called "Alzheimer's," and they also learned to grasp, with alarm, that people suffering from this disease were often only in their fifties, or even younger!

"If roses grow in Heaven Lord, then pick a bunch for me. Please place them in my mother's arms and tell her they're from me. Tell her that I love and miss her and when she turns to smile, place a kiss upon her cheek and hold her for awhile."

—Unknown Author

Submitted by Memory People member N Jane Bigham

Chapter 4

When Working as an Emergency Medical Technician

First off, I need you to understand that Rick has lived in the same area of Ohio all of his life. He never needed a road map, a GPS, or even an occasional stop at a gas station to ask directions. He knew every nook and cranny, landmark and even had a sense for what the traffic would be like at any given time of day. So obviously, when he first began to experience becoming lost in his own hometown, he understandably became concerned.

For twenty-four years Rick had been working as an Emergency Medical Technician (EMT) and loving every minute of it. This wasn't just a job to this man; he met each day with enthusiasm, ready to face whatever challenges lay ahead. This chosen profession was a beloved passion of his life; not only his alone, but also shared by his wife, Phyllis June, who is still currently working the same occupation, twenty-five years and counting.

As Rick's symptoms worsened, he continuously raised his concerns to Phyllis June and his fellow coworkers. He began receiving well-intentioned remarks like, "Rick, you're okay, it's just a phase." He wanted to believe his family and friends, but the fact of the matter was denial was surrounding him everywhere. What he did recollect as being a true comfort, however, was that he always had a coworker with him on duty, helping him to stay on track. I believe his biggest blessing was that he had been doing the job for such a long time, it became like second nature to him.

One day, as the driver of the ambulance on a long-distance nonemergency run transporting a patient to a local hospital they had been to hundreds of times before, his colleague suddenly asked him, "Rick, where are you going?" Realizing he had missed the hospital emergency entrance, he turned the rig around only to drive by it again and again. A rising sense of panic overwhelmed him.

Rick's mind was in a whirl. All along he had tried to discuss his concerns about his eroding condition with his coworkers, but these people were like family, some the best of friends. They all meant well, telling him, "Rick come on. Really, this is nothing to worry about." He wished he could embrace their beliefs, making them his own, but he knew he had to face up to the truth; things were only going to get worse.

This is one of the major problems with this disease. Everyone that surrounds the person who is suffering from it seems to be in some kind of denial. I've always said that denial is one symptom of Alzheimer's that affects everybody.

One Of those Days

Have you ever had one of those days?
When you should have stayed in bed,
When you put shampoo on your toothbrush,
Instead of on your head,
When your false teeth just don't fit,
And they don't feel as if they`re yours,
And all you want to do all day,
Is walk through different doors,
When your jumpers on inside out,
And stuck above your head,
When nobody can find you,
As your sitting in your shed,
This is what dementia does,
To me and many others,
But we are in a special group,
My sisters and my brothers,
Some may face this daily,
But with head held high,
As we end our day with a smile,
And not a fearful cry

Written by Norm McNamara

Chapter 5

The Last Run

The next few months became more difficult for Rick. Forgetting addresses he normally would've found "with his eyes closed" so to speak, he had become too embarrassed to ask his colleagues for help. Now he found himself sometimes calling his wife and asking *her* for directions.

On the nights prior to a work shift he would become extremely restless. As the stress mounted he began to experience symptoms of being physically ill, even to the point of vomiting.

One particular morning, aside from his ongoing anxiety, he felt hopeful that this would be a better day than usual. He was assigned to work from one of the outlying stations in the county, and it was known for its lighter workload. With a welcome sense of relief he joined his partner in the basic morning routine of going over the equipment checklist, performing a safety check on their assigned rig and being certain it was not lacking in supplies.

All too soon they received the call; a four-year-old girl was reported to be down, experiencing seizures at a housing development in that part of the county.

Whenever a call comes in concerning children in danger, the heartbeat of even a seasoned EMT increases, immediately causing adrenaline to surge throughout his or her entire system. This was how it felt for Rick and his partner as they raced to render aid. They knew the house was about eight minutes away. Rick was in the passenger seat and his partner was driving. He found himself rehearsing through his mind all the usual procedures that would likely be needed. Silently he prayed that he wouldn't suffer from a memory lapse and forget to do something critical.

Turning onto the street of their destination, they saw a small crowd of waving and screaming people who were pointing to the house where the little girl apparently was. It was second nature to Rick as he quickly grabbed what is known as the "first-in-bag," containing the basic necessities used in treating a patient. As Rick and his partner turned to sprint toward the house, one nervous-looking gentleman in particular took the lead, running ahead of them and showing them the way, all the time informing them that the girl was in the front room and she wasn't breathing.

This changed everything. As they entered through the front door, they found the child lying supine (face up). The girl had a bluish cast. They immediately checked for a carotid pulse, at the same time listening for breath sounds. There was absolutely no sign of life.

In a case like this, the proper procedure is to do what's called a "load-n-go." In an instant Rick gathered the equipment back into its bag as his partner lifted the four-year-old into his arms. Together they rushed to the truck where they continued to work chest compressions, also intubating the girl in order to supply needed oxygen.

The scene surrounding the ambulance was becoming chaotic. The child's parents were crying, neighbors and curious onlookers were everywhere, and tensions were rising.

Rick hopped on the radio and called for another ambulance to assist and also for a deputy. Emotions were running high and a calming voice of authority may be needed to prevent any further incident.

Running around to the back of the rescue unit and jumping in, he assured everyone watching that everything possible was being done. He closed up and secured the doors. They continued to supply oxygen and administer chest compressions. Still nothing! The decision was made for Rick to take off for the hospital, lights flashing and siren screaming. About three minutes down the road they met up with the other paramedics who quickly jumped in the back with Rick's partner and continued performing life-saving techniques on the child.

Rick radioed ahead to the hospital, apprising them of the seriousness of the situation. Upon arrival they lifted the child, still in the cot, and rushed her into the emergency room. They all stood watching as the hospital staff worked intently on the four-year-old girl. Finally, Rick couldn't stand it anymore. He told his partner, "That's enough for me," and he hurried outside to be alone, trying to gather his wits about him before anyone saw him shaking.

Hoping that familiarity would calm him, he began cleaning the truck for the next run but instead he found himself unable to do even that. His nerves were completely shot. He stood outside of the ambulance and lit up a cigarette and yelled out loud at himself, "What the hell am I trying to prove!"

"A real friend is one who walks in when the rest of the world walks out."

—Walter Winchell

Submitted by Memory People member Leeanne Chames

Chapter 6

A Defining Moment

Rick walked down to the end of the short ramp of the emergency entrance driveway to smoke a cigarette, attempting to get a hold of himself. As he plopped down on a bench he suddenly noticed his sister, pulling her car up to the curb. Knowing him the way she did, she only had to glance at him and saw that something was wrong. She threw her car in park and hurried over to where he was sitting. When she asked what was wrong, he assured her that he was okay, that they had just come off a bad run, and left it at that. He wasn't ready to talk about what had just happened. They said their goodbyes and I love yous. He watched her drive out of sight and, when he was certain he was alone again, he dug his cell phone out of his pocket and called his wife. With his voice revealing shattered emotions, he choked out the words that he didn't think he could do this anymore! He believed the time had come to end this madness before someone got seriously hurt! "I would never be able to forgive myself," he whispered.

Hanging up the phone, he looked toward the emergency entrance knowing that he would eventually have to make his way back inside. Taking a deep breath he slowly made his way toward the door, knowing all the while that there were two people he hoped he could avoid, the girl's parents. But this was not to be. Only minutes after re-entering the hospital he caught sight of a doctor informing them that everything possible had been done; and, sadly, they hadn't been able to save the little girl's life. Their precious daughter was gone!

It goes without saying; dealing with death is a dreadful thing. But when it involves the death of a young child, the pain is magnified incalculably.

Hearing the words of the doctor and the subsequent sobs of the parents was once again more than Rick could take! He desperately needed some fresh air. Rushing back outside he leaned his forehead against the coolness of the hospital's concrete wall. Fighting back tears and attempting to be invisible, Rick soon heard the sound of the sliding doors of the emergency exit, and there they were—the brokenhearted parents he had so hoped to avoid. As soon as the father saw Rick he said something to his wife and turned and made his way quickly toward him. Rick knew from experience that this could turn into a very ugly scene. He began thinking "okay, here we go." He figured the man was either going to walk up and punch him in the mouth or hug him.

As the distraught father approached him, Rick struggled to find his voice, expressing his deepest sympathies and how truly sorry he was for their loss. "We tried everything we could. We just couldn't revive her." The father grabbed Rick's hand and shook it saying, "I know you did." He pulled Rick close and hugged him. They both had tears streaming down their cheeks.

"A true friend is someone who sees the pain in your eyes while everyone else believes the smile on your face."

—Unknown Author

Submitted by Memory People member Liz Ridding

Chapter 7

The Debriefing

After enduring a heartbreaking experience such as the death of a child, emergency workers have the option of attending what is called a "Critical Care Incident Debriefing." Throughout his long career as an EMT, Rick had never gone to one. Despite all of the devastating runs he had been on, he never felt the urge, until now. He just couldn't shake the sorrow of the death of the little girl.

As Rick and his partner walked into the meeting the first thing they noticed were three familiar faces: the two nurses and the doctor who had attended to the little girl in the emergency room. They were sitting on folding chairs which were arranged in a circle. Among them also sat the counselor. The two men joined the group and listened as the counselor asked if there was anything in particular anyone wished to discuss. The room fell silent. Soon, with gentle encouragement, those in attendance began to open up. They felt a sense of relief as they discussed how hard this case had been. Not one of them could understand how, with all their expertise, knowledge, and high-tech equipment, "something like this could still happen?" The discussion was a much-needed release for the attendees and went on as long as was necessary.

As the session eventually came to a close, Rick asked the counselor if it would be okay if they spoke privately afterward. His partner patted him on the shoulder and told him he'd be waiting outside and to take his time.

The advisor was sure that Rick wanted to simply discuss his grief brought on by the child's death. Instead, the man was shocked when Rick told him "I'm positive I didn't do anything wrong to cause what happened to the girl, but what if something had happened due to the lapse of memory I've been suffering lately. I can't go through this again!" Rick could see the man was shocked and was beginning to listen to him with greater concern. He was heartened as he thought, for the first time, maybe he had found someone who was truly hearing him! As they finished this emotionally draining discussion, Rick asked the counselor if he could please call his wife. He was exhausted. He whispered, "I just need to go home."

It wasn't long before Rick saw Phyllis June pulling up in front of the hospital where the meeting had been held. He walked outside and saw his partner standing there, still waiting for him. With concern in his voice, he asked, "Are you okay, Rick?" "No, I'm not. I'm going home." His partner agreed that would probably be best. As Rick dropped into the passenger seat of his wife's car, the counselor made his way up to the driver's window and told Phyllis June that Rick was having a hard time with dealing with the child's death and to call him if they needed anything. Rick's first thoughts were "I should have known better. To actually think someone was finally listening to me."

After a couple of unspoken miles, Phyllis June eventually asked him, "So what's going on?" He told her "I'm done! I've been trying to explain this to you, and to everybody else. Nobody seems to get it. I can't do this anymore. That was, without a doubt, my last run being an EMT."

Arriving home, Phyllis June stayed with him for a couple of hours until she had to go back to work. Rick knew he had to do something. Talk with his family practitioner again? Yes. That was the one thing he was sure of; it was time to see his doctor again, put his foot down, and demand they all get to the bottom of this.

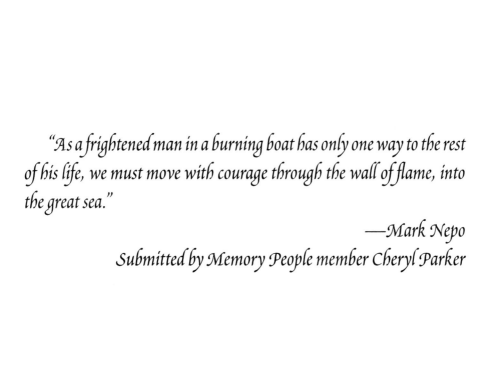

"As a frightened man in a burning boat has only one way to the rest of his life, we must move with courage through the wall of flame, into the great sea."

—Mark Nepo
Submitted by Memory People member Cheryl Parker

Chapter 8

The Next Step

Every morning as he watched his wife head off to work, there was a tear in Rick's soul. He knew how desperately they needed that second income. They had always planned on it being there.

Finding himself alone, the house began closing in on him. Over and over he would forget the reason why he was home and not at work. His mind was in a whirl.

Now that he had finally been diagnosed with Early-Onset Alzheimer's disease, the reality of never being able to do his job again as an EMT began to sink in even deeper. Thankfully, Rick had three months worth of sick days built up, so he was officially placed on "sick leave" by the county. Nevertheless, that time was quickly dissipating. What a relief it was when his faithful coworkers found out the news of his diagnosis and pulled together, donating another thirty days of their own personal sick leave to him! They were indeed like family.

Rick attempted to cash in his public employment

retirement savings but was quickly told that this wasn't an option. He was still legally considered an employee.

That night he asked Phyllis June if she could drive him to the squad house in the morning so he could officially resign. She sat down next to him and asked "Are you sure you want to do this? It just seems so final." "Yes," he told her. "We have to be realistic about this. I'll never be able to do this job again. I'm only going to get worse." He explained how he tried to get his retirement savings and they wouldn't release it. "We're running out of money! We've been a two-income family forever. I would hate to think that if we lost our house, it would be because of me."

They decided that she would drive him down on her lunch break the following day. What they didn't expect to find out was that even after resigning for medical reasons, his retirement funds wouldn't be released for another three months.

For Rick, this wasn't like giving up just any job; there was something extremely rewarding about this career. After years of helping people day after day, he knew there had developed a space inside his soul where empathy had evolved into part of his own well-being. What would fill this space now?

One of the blessings Rick had throughout this period was how he treasured the moment when Phyllis June would return home from work. They would sit around and talk about her day. Even with Rick's dementia continually becoming worse, it was a subject that he could still relate to very well and it somehow brought him a sense of comfort.

They figured that the next step for them financially would be filing for "State Disability Income" (SSI).

"In the end, all that really matters is who you loved and who loved you."
—Unknown Author
Submitted by Memory People member Sheila Murff Brantley

Chapter 9

Filing for Disability

As the family's financial situation continued to deteriorate, Rick decided to call the local Social Security office and explain his need to file for disability. Eventually, he received a package in the mail containing paperwork that was necessary to be filled out in order to start his claim. Looking through the forms, his first thought was that he would be able to complete them himself. This turned out to be the farthest thing from the truth. There were ten pages of questions that would have been confusing for a person who *wasn't* suffering from dementia.

That same evening Phyllis June sat down with him, and together they spent more than three hours on the documents. Finally they had everything completed and ready to be mailed out the next morning.

A couple of weeks later they received a letter telling them good news; because Rick's claim stated that he was "memory-impaired," his case would be considered "fast-tracked." The Social Security Administration had passed an act, in February 2010, to speed up the process of those who are diagnosed with Early-Onset Alzheimer's. Prior to this, these people were unable to receive benefits until they finally reached the point where they were qualified for Medicare and Social Security at the age of sixty-five.

The next step along this long road was Rick receiving a phone call, asking if he would be willing to be tested by an Ohio State Physician. After accepting and waiting a two-week period, Rick and Phyllis June drove about forty miles to this appointment.

The doctor was a neurologist, a psychologist, and a psychiatrist all wrapped up into one. The testing lasted for three hours. It wasn't until the tests were completed that they were told that this physician wasn't the person who made the actual decision of whether Rick would be approved or not; this was the responsibility of the Social Security Office in Columbus, Ohio. The doctor's job was only to perform and send the test results to Columbus.

At the end of the day, Rick and Phyllis June had to leave the facility without any kind of confirmation as to whether or not he was going to receive any benefits. Needless to say, they drove home disappointed.

Fortunately, three weeks later they received the answer they were hoping for. They were overjoyed to find that Rick had been approved, but what they were surprised to learn was that they wouldn't receive their first payment for another six months.

To this day Rick will argue about what the state considers to be a "fast-tracked" process; as he then had to wait another twenty-four months before any medical insurance would kick in.

"Write your heartaches in sand and your Blessing in Stone."

—George Bernard Shaw

Submitted by Memory People member Margie Layman

Chapter 10

Meeting with an Attorney

In between waiting for his disability checks and the endless days of praying, Rick scheduled an appointment with an "Elder Law Attorney." There were matters of the utmost importance that needed to be addressed and, knowing that time was of the essence, the act of retaining a lawyer had to be performed immediately.

Before Rick even had a diagnosis of Alzheimer's, he and Phyllis June had been discussing having a "Last Will and Testament" drawn up. Now there was a sense of urgency about it, leaving no more time to procrastinate. Documents had to be signed while Rick was still considered legally capable.

After agreeing on an attorney that specialized in elder issues, the appointment was made to coincide with Phyllis June's lunch break. Arriving first, Rick sat by a window waiting patiently. He watched as his wife parked the car. A feeling of warmth came over him, realizing that he would never have to go through this campaign alone.

He deeply loved and admired her, watching as she walked up the sidewalk.

When at last they sat in the attorney's meeting room, Rick explained to him that he was very recently diagnosed with Early-Onset Alzheimer's disease. "We're worried about how this is going to affect our financial future."

The attorney sat across from them at his desk, taking notes on a yellow legal pad. He asked several questions about Early-Onset Alzheimer's, indicating that, like most of the general public, he lacked awareness about this disease. His main query was what did they think the future was going to hold for them. Rick told him "Well it's not going to be good; in fact for me it is terminal. In time I will most likely end up in an adult living facility."

He went on to say that currently Phyllis June was paying all the bills and had been for quite some time. "Actually, I can't even remember the last time I even wrote a check. This is not our biggest concern. What we're really worried about is losing our home. When I do end up in a nursing home, I don't want the state coming after our house for reimbursement. We want to put the deed in Phyllis June's name only. I also want to make her my durable power of attorney, financially and medically. We would also like to have our wills drawn up."

They supplied all the documents that he requested, including their marriage license. Then they waited for their next appointment, which was in three weeks.

Upon their return, the attorney explained that there was one major problem he foresaw: since they still owed money on the house, there was a possibility that the bank may notice the deed transfer in the public announcements of the local newspaper. If so, they might contest the transaction. "You have the option of notifying them or just rolling the dice." They both thought about it for a short minute and decided to roll them.

They were informed that their vehicles wouldn't be a problem. They would automatically go into Phyllis June's name when Rick's time came. If something unforeseen happened to Phyllis June and she died first, everything would go back into Rick's name and their daughter would become the second beneficiary. Rick also had a living will drawn up, stating his wishes, including a Do Not Resuscitate/Comfort Care order (DNRCC).

The land transfer was published without being disputed. One thing they discovered later on was that they were now unable to claim a tax break on their property taxes for Rick's disability, since the house was now in Phyllis June's ownership.

The following are some questions to ask an attorney regarding planning for the future:

- How can we plan to completely avoid probate upon the event of both our deaths?
- Are we eligible for Medicaid now if we need it?
- Do we have complete powers under our POA to handle Medicaid planning, asset protection, gifting, income, gift and estate tax planning and perform probate avoidance planning?
- How can we protect our home and savings and other assets from nursing home and uncovered medical expenses?
- Are we subject to any state or federal estate taxes on both of our deaths?
- Do we need to do any income tax planning?

- Do we have both primary and contingent beneficiaries on our life insurance, annuities, and IRAs so as to avoid probate if our primary beneficiary dies first?
- Are our life insurance proceeds protected in case of the death of one of us, if the survivor goes into a nursing home?
- Do we have any excess resources for Medicaid purposes and if so how do we protect them?
- If one of us goes into a nursing home, how much will we have to pay the nursing home if we are on Medicaid and how much monthly income will the healthy spouse have left to live on?
- Is there a HIPPA waiver for our health care proxy?
- Do we have a living will?
- What if one of our children predeceases us? How can we make provisions for a trust for our grandchildren?
- If one of our children gets divorced, gets disabled, gets a judgment or a tax lien against them, or goes bankrupt, does that affect assets we've gifted to them? Does it affect our home?
- If our house is in an Irrevocable Trust, will there be a tax if we sell it?
- If a child or grandchild has estranged themselves from the family, how do we cut them out of our will?
- Can we avoid a will?

So Brave

I will never forget that awful day, When dementia came to take you away, All those memories, all those years, Running down my face, now as tears, Why is this life, oh so cruel, Trying to turn you into Dementia's fool, But above it all, you stood tall, When dementia, came to call, Every day you stood and fought, So determined, not to be caught, Its all this, we will remember, When looking back, on life's embers, How brave you were in dementia's Face, Never slowing to its pace, So goodbye my love, see you soon, On the bright side of the moon

Written by Norm McNamara

Chapter 11

The Perfect Storm

Each day, as Rick opens his eyes from what sleep he has been able to come by, a feeling of uselessness, born of this disease, crushes him. Mix this together with a tired, run-down feeling, the anxiety that stems from feeling lost and disoriented throughout the day, along with just plain fear, and he has what I would consider to be a "perfect storm."

You may think that after dealing with the memory issues for as long as Rick already has, that he might be somewhat accustomed to it. Unfortunately, Alzheimer's doesn't work that way.

Daily, Rick feels himself slipping away. He's endlessly losing his yesterdays and is relentlessly worried about losing his tomorrows as well. Everything is becoming more difficult for him; he used to know ahead of time when a bad day was coming his way, but now they just crash down on him! The bad spells are coming upon him more and more aggressively and, unfortunately, they're lasting longer.

In the beginning months of walking this difficult journey, Rick would sense a dark cloud of confusion beginning to shadow over him. At times, when this began to take him over, he would immediately take his dogs for a walk and attempt to clear his head; if nothing else, at least the fresh air felt good. Now, however, he comes home from these walks with what seems like as overcast sky ready to burst open and pour down upon his head.

As I write this, Rick is considered to only be in the early-to-mid stage of the disease; but he's already having multiple difficulties coping with everyday life. What does this say about the future? It's frightening, to say the least, but he's determined to communicate to the public as much awareness and guidance as possible about Alzheimer's and the world of EOAD.

Throughout the next part of this book, I'm going to attempt to describe the hardships of Rick's everyday life. I will be drawing from the experience of being my father's caregiver for ten years, keeping him home with me until he took his final breath, dying from Alzheimer's himself. Sadly, I know all too well which direction this disease takes.

Like my father was, Rick is a strong individual. I see the same fight in Rick that my dad had all the way to his finish line. But in the end, it's the Alzheimer's that always wins.

"I have heard there are troubles of more than one kind. Some come from ahead and some from behind. But I've brought a big bat. I'm all ready you see. Now my troubles are going to have trouble with me!"

—Dr. Seuss

Submitted by Amy Reierson

Chapter 12

The "On" Switch

Alzheimer's Disease seems to have a switch that turns itself off and on at any given moment. It is common for people with Alzheimer's to be having an upbeat day when suddenly, out of nowhere, a rogue wave of anxiety washes over them.

Rick tells of a time when he, his wife, and their niece decided to go to a new hamburger joint for its grand opening. This turned out to be a huge mistake. The place was slammed! There was a long wait for a table, and they found themselves stuck in the thick of a crowd. Trying not to panic, Rick did his best to keep his mind focused on the simple reality of where he was, telling himself that they would have a table opening up for them at any moment.

Unfortunately, some well-meaning friends of theirs made their way over to them and began the typical conversation that Rick was now becoming accustomed to: "How have you been, Rick? We heard about you being diagnosed with Alzheimer's. That's just unbelievable.

You look so good." On and on went the chatting and the questions. Doing everything he could think of to keep himself together, Rick tried to take it in stride. As time passed more patrons continued coming into the already cramped waiting area, and the noise kept getting louder. There was commotion everywhere! In the middle of the conversation, Rick suddenly excused himself and quickly exited the restaurant.

(Scared stiff in the middle of the day in a room full of people? This may sound crazy, but this is only one of the many ways this horrific disease can torment its victims.)

Phyllis June came running out after him. She could see fear written all over his face. "Rick, are you okay?" "No!" he answered in a shaky voice, "I need to go home."

Once again he found himself on the couch lying down! He hated so much to do this during the middle of the day when he felt that he should be doing something productive. Now, on his back, staring at the ceiling, guilt started to overwhelm him.

He and his wife had so few opportunities to do things together. They had finally had a chance but, instead they had to come home early because he couldn't handle it. She had been working herself to death, six days a week, worried about him every minute she was away. Rick could see the worry etched on her face, but she always kept telling him that everything was going to be okay. It's just so unfair! He laid there as the tears began to flow.

After his diagnosis he and Phyllis June had been told, by the experts, that they would have to change their lifestyle. He lay there wondering, "Could this be what they meant?"

Almost overnight, they had gone from having two

incomes to one. But the bills kept coming in. The prescriptions still needed to be filled. The list goes on and on and is very sad.

Rick has now learned to inform others that "If you think you're financially well off, you may want to think again." This disease has more time and patience than you most likely have money. Whatever assets you had before this pilfering demon strikes will be drained.

Unfortunately, there is precious little financial help for caregivers and to make matters worse, most of them will eventually have to give up their employment. This is something that desperately needs to be changed. Rick has said many times that "caregivers are not asking for a hand out, just a hand up."

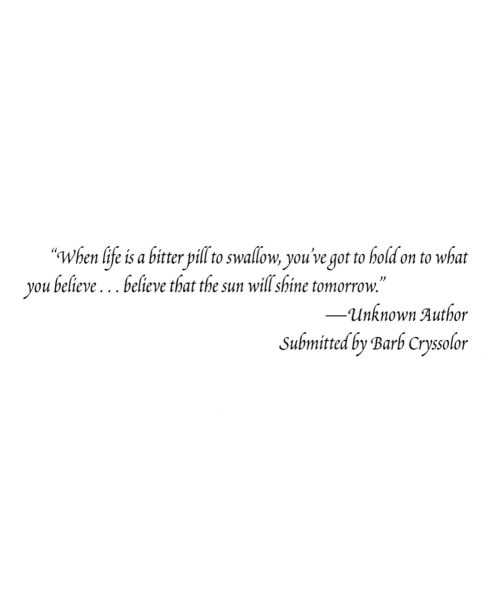

"When life is a bitter pill to swallow, you've got to hold on to what you believe . . . believe that the sun will shine tomorrow."

—Unknown Author

Submitted by Barb Cryssolor

Chapter 13

Remembering to Take Medications

After several mishaps and many anxious days of not knowing if Rick had taken his medication properly, Phyllis June went to the local drugstore and bought a pill dispenser with separate compartments, clearly marked for different times of each day.

The purpose behind this was twofold: to alleviate some confusion on Rick's part and also so that she could track whether or not he had missed any doses. Before this change, Rick would often walk by and stare at the pills that she had laid out for him that day, but it would not always register with him to actually take them. Phyllis June would arrive home from work only to find the little pile of pills exactly where she had placed them earlier.

Also, another scenario that had been familiar before the change was that, at night, she would place both hers and Rick's medications on the kitchen counter. Rick would go into the fridge to get himself a glass of cold water, but by the time the water was to the top of the glass the thought of taking his pills had completely vanished from his mind. After he made his way to the bedroom, Phyllis June would ask him if he had taken his pills. Rick simply did not know and would have to go back out to the kitchen to check. No, this didn't happen every single night, but it was occurring much too often.

Another struggle had been with Rick's Exelon patch, which had been prescribed for him to wear daily. After showering, he would open the box to replace the one he had removed before the shower and frequently, he would find two or three patches from days before which he had obviously forgotten to remove.

Here is a good tip to follow: Write the date right on the patch when it's being administered, using a marker or pen. This may help to keep things on track by knowing if it's yesterday's dosage or not.

The bottom line here is that patients suffering from Alzheimer's will eventually need supervision handling their medications. Throughout the years of caring for my father it was always an on-again-off-again battle keeping his medication on track. I can't count the amount of times I heard him say "I already took my pills" when they were still sitting right in front of him.

"Don't regret yesterday, it is the perfect compass guiding your journey today."

—Unknown Author

Submitted by Memory People member Kathy Guess

Chapter 14

That Lost Feeling

Lately, Rick has been undergoing a very unpleasant new symptom: he has the perception of being lost. He says, without a doubt, that it is one of the toughest things that he has been through yet; and it's with him endlessly, every day, even in the safety and familiarity of his own home.

This feeling of being lost always seems to be accompanied with a sensation of loneliness. Together they embody an eerie feeling of being watched.

Why does this happen? Rick will tell you, "That's the million-dollar question." It's as if there's a shadow always hanging over his shoulders. His only explanation is a familiar one, "It's the disease. It's always the disease!"

Gardening with Alzheimer's

As I sit here in my garden, wondering what to do,
Trying to remember the flowers names, and the roses too,
Remembering all those days gone by,
Endless summers and clear blue sky,
Knowing all the names, of course in Latin as well,
Now it's which is which, Far too hard to tell,
Watching all the flowers dance,
Roses sway, pansies prance,
Some names will stay with me, I hope for all my life,
But some I will forget, amongst the mist and strife
And until that day arrives, when I remember none,
Endless summers and blue skies gone,
I will continue to plant till my heart's content,
Because all Earths flowers are heaven sent.

Written by Norm McNamara

Chapter 15

The Cocoon Effect

Every day Rick wakes up wondering, "Is this going to be another bad day?" He tries in vain to escape these thoughts. To accomplish such a feat would be the equivalent of being able to think of absolutely nothing.

The many emotions that evolve from this disease are: loneliness, anger, apathy, fear, and an odd feeling of becoming hollow. That's just to name a few. At times, Rick doesn't even understand how he manages to endure them. Dealing with these emotions all at once and also the uncertainty of how long they're going to last brings a level of anxiety to him that is certainly hard to regulate on his own.

Early-Onset Alzheimer's Disease has affected Rick in a host of different ways. It has altered him as a whole person, including changing his personality and behaviors. I'm not saying this in a bad way, but he now lives a more cautious life.

His conversations have changed, especially with

strangers. Before, he always loved being around people, but now it has become upsetting. He can handle it for only short periods of time, but after a while it becomes too difficult for him to maintain his equanimity. Just the thought of knowing he will soon be around a group of people puts him on edge.

When out in public he worries about the confusion of running into someone that might know him. Does he truly know that person? Should he say hello or just walk by? He cannot distinguish between these people being friends from the past or new acquaintances. Sadly, he finds himself staring down at his shoes a lot. He calls this the "elevator syndrome."

There are times when everything feels as if it is closing in on him. It's as if the disease itself has wrapped around him like a cocoon.

His mind starts to drift and then race about 100 mph, moving so fast that he cannot concentrate on a single thought. These troubled spells are fueled by the worry of wondering, "How long are they going to last? A couple of hours or maybe a couple of days?" All of this mental anguish can increase the length of time that the troubles persist.

During these episodes he constantly wants to call Phyllis June at work, but he tries to refrain, knowing he can't keep disturbing her. Instead, he once again lies down and tries to sleep, attempting to ride out the storm.

"Go back and take care of yourself. Your body needs you, your feelings need you, your perceptions need you. Your suffering needs you to acknowledge it. Go home and be there for all these things . . ."

—Thich Nhat Hanh

Submitted by Memory People member Ruth Boshart

Chapter 16

Restless Nights

Rick doesn't remember how long ago it started, but he's been struggling with nighttime woes for quite a while. He fights sleep disorders almost every night, sleeping for only three to four hours at best. Naturally, exhaustion sets in during the middle of the next day. This much lack of sleep would deeply intensify anyone's confusion. Place that on the top of someone who has Alzheimer's, and it can become an awfully rough ride.

I have always believed that when Alzheimer's patients' sleep patterns become disrupted, this is usually a sign that they are advancing into yet another stage of the disease. Rick has heard over and over, "try to just lay there, you'll fall back to sleep eventually." What people don't understand is that, with this disease, attempting to just lay there can induce a super stress mode. His thoughts start racing to places like: worrying about the future and what disabilities may lie ahead for him, visions of the devastation this disease is going to cause for Phyllis June and his family, etc. Add all of these thoughts to the basic fact that he is faced with a fatal disease, and his thoughts become almost demonic for him.

During the few hours of sleep he *does* receive, he is overcome with horrific nightmares. Often, Rick wakes up kicking and jerking in a wild panic; his bed is soaked from cold sweats, and he's shaking all over, battling his overwhelming confusion. It may actually be a blessing that he never remembers what these disturbing dreams are about.

Occurring on almost a nightly basis, it's nearly as though he's hallucinating in his sleep. This may literally be the case.

After he's awake for about fifteen minutes, he finally gets himself oriented to his surroundings, realizing that he's in the safety of his own home.

Rick and Phyllis June have talked to several of his physicians about this problem. One doctor asked if he was sure they were nightmares. Rick told him, "Not really." Then Phyllis June jumped into the conversation and explained how he would sometimes let out frightful screams. The doctor tweaked his medication and, once again, they were out the door. Did the nightmares stop? Unfortunately, no.

Rick tries to stay up as late as possible, so that when hopefully he *does* hit the bed, he'll be tired enough to fall asleep right away but, as if he has an internal alarm clock ticking inside, he will most likely awaken in the middle of the night.

Quietly getting up and trying not to disturb his wife, he sometimes opens the front door to breathe in some fresh air, staring enviously out at a sleeping neighborhood. He wonders how long this is going to last. "Is this only a phase I'm going through?"

Rick feels deep empathy for those who are in the advanced stage of this disease. What if they're also having nightmares and are unable to express to anyone what they're going through?

These nights are exhausting for him, and they naturally force him to take a nap during the day. Unfortunately, there are times where he actually feels worse after awakening from these catnaps.

You know for a fact that this disease has altered your life when you start dreading bedtime.

"*Life is not the way it is supposed to be . . . it's the way it is . . . the way we cope with it, is what makes the difference.*"

—*Unknown Author*

Submitted by Memory People member Phyllis June Phelps

Chapter 17

Losing the Ability to Read

Prior to starting this book, I asked Rick if he could make a list of things that were now sadly missing in his life. He did just that and near the top of the list was reading.

He hasn't been able to comprehend what he reads for over a year now. This dilemma actually began for him three or four years ago. His reading comprehension of anything more than just two paragraphs dwindled away. By the time he would move on to a third paragraph, recollections of what he'd already taken in had dissipated.

This is the reason why Rick has specifically asked me to keep the chapters short throughout this book. It is his desire that those who are in the early stages of this disease will still be able to read this book and absorb the content, thus learning from his experiences.

I know that even as a caregiver it is quite difficult to sit down and read the daily newspaper. Between the high levels of stress and the constant worry about loved ones afflicted with Alzheimer's, this transforms any "down time" into a difficult task.

Phyllis June now reads everything to her husband; even the drafts that I sent them from this book. Rick patiently waits for her to read them to him, so they can both discuss the subject matter of each chapter.

While caring for my dad, I noticed that he would only read the first five pages of a book or sometimes he would just pick up at whatever page he happened to open it to. It got to the point where he would sit for long periods of time and just stare at the front page of the newspaper.

As an author and columnist, not being able to read would be like tying my hands behind my back. I would have to clarify it as a disability in and of itself.

"They invented hugs to let people know you love them without saying anything."

—Bill Keene

Submitted by Rick Phelps, Founder of Memory People

Chapter 18

Sundowner's

Sundown Syndrome, also known as Sundowner's, is a term describing the onset of heavier confusion and intensified agitation. Usually, this begins anywhere from late afternoon to dusk, but in reality, it could happen anytime during the day.

Rick believes it sometimes affects him during the morning hours. I noticed that my dad suffered from it especially throughout dreary rainy days, filled with dark overcast skies.

As Sundowner's advances upon him, Rick usually notices himself starting to pace. Sometimes he also experiences a twitching in his legs, similar to "restless leg syndrome." Even the sound of a single spoon falling to the kitchen floor is amplified as if someone has dropped the whole drawer of silverware. Lately, he has noticed that even the sound of his dog's toenails clicking across the hardwood floor is becoming extremely disturbing.

Sometimes his heightened sensitivity can last well into

the night. During these periods, Rick finds himself verbally rambling on, constantly asking Phyllis June, "What are we doing?"

During the Christmas season, they went shopping for presents at the mall in the early afternoon. As usual, this took much longer than anticipated. Rick could sense the shadow of Sundowner's approaching him. Once again he found himself outside in search of some fresh air. A mass amount of cars were driving around, trying to find a place to park. Rick felt as if he had walked out onto the streets of New York City.

When a person experiences Sundown Syndrome, everything becomes highly magnified. Experts believe that one of the contributing factors is a shift in the biological clock, caused by the change from daylight to darkness. A good preventive step is to make sure all the lights are turned on throughout the house a good hour before it becomes dark, keeping any shadows from creeping into the home.

Rick and I both believe that the onset of this syndrome also has a lot to do with the end-of-day exhaustion. Dealing with the symptoms of Alzheimer's all day long would wear anyone down by the evening hours, enhancing anxiety and confusion.

At my house, around 4:45 p.m., everyone got a new name. I learned to become proactive, keeping my father entertained with a photo album or I would sometimes pick up the cat and place her on my dad's lap, telling him that the cat was lonely. By the time the cat began to purr, Dad would once again become calm. There's definitely something to be said for pet therapy.

If you are a caregiver and you know what time of day this syndrome usually attacks, try to be prepared ahead of time. It's easier to divert your loved one's confusion early on than after it is too advanced.

Christmas Shopping

Just been shopping for Christmas stuff,
Watching wives and husbands going off in a huff,
Heavy breathing and bright red faces,
Like human horses going through the races,
Children screaming, mummies shouting,
Teenagers in Debenhams with mouths pouting,
Dads in the pub with their mates,
Ordering pints and take away crates,
Then there's me, in the middle of this,
Needing a hug and a little kiss,
Watching my wallet emptying fast,
How long will this Christmas last?
Then it's time for home, a little bit lighter,
And not just my wallet that I grab tighter,
Because it's too late, my moneys all gone,
Still, at least, the shopping is done!!

Written by Norm McNamara

Chapter 19

Holiday Sacrifices

Keeping loved ones in a daily routine is essential. Family members and caregivers must realize this as early in their campaign as possible. I believe this is truly the number one rule caregivers should follow, in order to keep their loved ones as calm as feasible. This way everyone's quality of life is better.

This past Christmas, Rick and Phyllis June came to the conclusion that putting up a tree or decorating for the holidays would be too much for him to handle anymore.

When friends and relatives hear of this, they usually ask in disbelief, "How can you not have a Christmas tree?" Well, it's not as if Rick has a phobia of trees or anything. It's just that the blinking lights and the rearranging of the furniture upsets him.

It is truly disturbing to take someone who is suffering from Alzheimer's disease out of their routine. One might ask how moving furniture around can upset someone's routine. Well, when I was caring for my dad, if I put a new painting on the wall or moved a clock, he would believe some stranger had snuck in and changed the whole house around. There were times I couldn't even convince him he was even in our own home. Trust me; it was better to leave things as they were, just keeping his confusion level to a low.

Rick and Phyllis June knew that their grandchildren would be sadly disappointed when visiting, not to see the house glistening with Christmas season decorations. But when families are dealing with dementia of any kind, many traditions have to be put aside for the time being while they and their loved ones fight this dreaded disease.

Try to hold the family celebrations in a familiar environment, like their own home. Taking afflicted ones to another family member's dwelling could prove to be too confusing for them. This could end up devastating everyone's holiday.

Once guests have arrived in the home, refrain from having everyone visit with the patients all at once. Talk with the family ahead of time, keeping the traffic to a minimum. If possible, try to make up a schedule for when they should visit. Attempting to recognize too many faces at once or listen to the sounds of multiple voices all talking at the same time will become extremely upsetting.

Another rule of thumb is to try to limit gatherings to the daytime hours only. Visiting at night, when mental confusion is much more pronounced, will be extremely difficult for them.

I'm not telling you to give up on celebrating your holidays. Instead, make a plan in advance so that your family can still experience the fullest enjoyment without making it too exhausting on your loved ones and on you, the caregiver.

"You never know how strong you are, until being strong is the only choice you have."

—Unknown Author

Submitted by Memory People member Ann Collins

Chapter 20

That Dreaded Cell Phone

Rick used to own a BlackBerry Storm cell phone that he absolutely loved. One morning he woke up and realized he had completely forgotten how to operate the thing. He was even having problems trying to figure out how to answer something as simple as incoming calls.

He kept this secret to himself for quite a while as he was too embarrassed to tell anyone, including his wife. Finally, he confessed his burden to Phyllis June. They decided to go out and purchase a very basic, easy-to-operate flip cell phone; no bells and whistles. In spite of its simplicity, Rick had a hard time even comprehending how to turn this one on. The ability to learn new things with this disease can be flat out impossible.

Having previously purchased an IPad, Rick was accustomed to its format, so he decided to give an iPhone a try. The basics were the same, and he seemed to operate this phone like it was second nature.

He was able to e-mail, text, and search the Internet

with the iPhone almost instantly. It has worked so well for him that now he has upgraded to a new version of that phone. It has what is called a "personal assistant" built right in. He can literally speak into the phone, asking it almost any question, and the phone speaks back to him.

For example, "What day is it?" The phone replies, "Today is Tuesday, November 29th ." He can also record a to-do list or set up a system of reminders. (I think I could even use a phone like that!)

The best part of all is that his iPhone is also equipped with a "find me" program.

Phyllis June can enter a password into *her* phone and a GPS locator will tell her exactly where Rick is. That is, provided he has the phone with him.

For Rick, this has worked out great as it is "user friendly" for him but also, as I stated before, he was already accustomed to this kind of format.

This disease can take away the ability to learn even the simplest of new techniques, so use caution. If you do decide to switch phones for loved ones who are memory impaired, use the same carrier or at least make sure they can retain the same phone number they already had. If not, I guarantee they'll be constantly giving out the old number.

Here are my friends they hold not my hand,
Sometimes I know who they are and where they stand.
They make me laugh when I am down,
They bring me up and wipe away my frown.
We all shine bright in our own way,
We watch out for each other that's how it will stay.
Some of us are tired a few a little wired,
But give us a chance to help baggage required.
Written by Amy Reierson

Chapter 21

The Fifty-Question Greeting

Everyone who knows Rick personally is aware that he has been diagnosed with Early-Onset Alzheimer's Disease. Not only has he been on the radio many times trying to bring awareness to the illness, he's also been the subject of several articles on the front page of his local newspaper. In addition, he and Phyllis June live in a small community where news travels at lightning speed.

People definitely treat him differently now that he has this disease. Rick calls it the "fifty-question greeting." Well-meaning folks completely bombard him with questions when they see him and, truthfully, that's one of the worst things to do to someone who is suffering from Alzheimer's.

Friends perpetually ask how he's doing, and the honest answer to that question is "Probably worse than the last time you saw me." This disease constantly forges its way down a one-way street.

There's a local pub fairly close to where Rick and Phyllis June live where they used to enjoy visiting maybe once a month or so. Although she doesn't drink, Phyllis June would drive Rick and herself down there so he could enjoy having a couple of beers with the guys; if nothing else it gave him a little taste of a normal social life. These are people that they have known for years, including the owner.

Sadly, Rick can no longer handle crowds, which at this point can be more than two people at a time. So if they do go, it's usually during the early afternoon when the place is half deserted.

As sociable people, they have always enjoyed mingling with friends and playing pool. They were social drinkers at best, always home early, then sitting down discussing their evening over a cup of coffee or tea.

But now, if Rick walks into the pub, he gets overwhelmed with "Rick, we haven't seen you forever." He's even been told that he's changed. "You're just not the same old 'Joe' you used to be." He always replies with "I'm still the same person and I always will be, but this disease has changed the way I have to function through my everyday life."

In essence, the general public does not understand the effects this disease has on an individual. It's not only a memory disorder, but there are also mental and physical disabilities involved here.

Rick understands the effect that alcohol has on his memory and realizes that he has enough difficulties to deal with as it is. He wants to preserve what time and memory he has left and does not want to aid in his memory impairment. He dearly misses socializing with his buddies, shooting the breeze, talking about the "good old days," etc.

This is just one more part of life that Alzheimer's will steal from its victims. The number of sacrifices that have to be made when fighting this illness is absolutely endless.

"A man's real possession is his memory. In nothing else is he rich, in nothing else is he poor."

—Alexander Smith

Submitted by Memory People member Charles Schoenfeld

Chapter 22

The Walmart Dilemma

Rick began to realize that every time he drove to the local Walmart store, he couldn't remember the process of driving there. To make matters worse, upon exiting the store, he could never remember where he parked his Jeep. Due to this dilemma he began parking as close to the front of the store as possible. Many of his friends gave advice such as placing an orange tennis ball on the top of his car antenna or pushing the panic button on his key chain, setting off an alarm. What people don't realize is that by that point, he was so worked up, he wouldn't even remember about the orange marker or even taking the keys out of his pocket.

He began to walk into the store consistently gripping a shopping list, which he desperately needed. Although this didn't always work out for him as planned, on one trip he went straight to the pet section and grabbed a fifty-pound bag of dog food. While picking up the bag, he placed his shopping list down. After loading the bag in his cart he began searching frantically for the paper, turning his pockets inside out, finding nothing. Panic set in. Deciding to try shopping by memory, he started roaming through the store only to be overwhelmed by that dark cloud of anxiety. He quickly paid for the dog food and exited the building. So ultimately, the only thing he brought home with him that was actually needed was the dog food!

Soon it became necessary to only go shopping when Phyllis June was available to accompany him. He would always follow her, pushing the cart, constantly keeping his hands on the handlebar. This acted as a security blanket for him. Occasionally, his wife would tell him that she had to go get some makeup or some other accessory. She would suggest, "Why don't you go get us some butter, milk, etc." He would quickly respond, "No way! I don't want to wander around all by myself." Sadly, Rick had developed a gripping fear of getting lost.

They always seemed to finish up their shopping at the deli department. One time in particular, Phyllis June told him she had forgotten the dishwashing soap. "Why don't you stay here in line and order the sandwich meat we need, I'll be back in two minutes, okay?" So off she went and, sure enough, they called his number. After nervously ordering what he hoped his wife wanted, he stood there waiting for what seemed an eternity.

(At this stage of the disease Rick had already lost his sense of time. What might actually be only two to three minutes to him felt like thirty to forty minutes or even longer.)

So now he's panicking, thinking something must have happened to her! He stood there becoming more agitated by the second. Finally, she came walking up and he practically yelled at her, "Where have you been? You've been gone forever!" She calmly told him, "Rick. I've only been gone a couple of minutes."

Ever since that day, he tries to never take his hands off the cart. He follows her around in the store faithfully. As embarrassing as this may be for him, with this terrible disease, it's just the way it has to be.

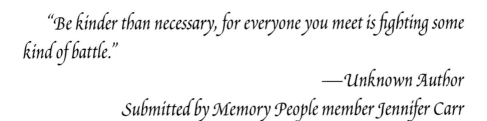

"Be kinder than necessary, for everyone you meet is fighting some kind of battle."

—Unknown Author

Submitted by Memory People member Jennifer Carr

Chapter 23

The Problems with Credit Cards

In recent times shopping on-line has certainly taken the world by storm. For most people it is incredibly easy and uncomplicated. Not so for Alzheimer's sufferers. Rick will attest to this.

Finding himself in need of khaki-colored Dockers style pants, he turned on the computer and began to browse. It didn't take long for him to locate the exact trousers he was looking for. Happily typing away, he filled out the order form with his correct size, etc. and, using his credit card, purchased three pairs to be shipped directly to his home address. After completing the order he felt extremely satisfied with himself. Within a week, UPS showed up at his front door with two very large boxes. Seeing that his name was on the packages, he immediately signed for them. Upon opening them, however, he instantly wondered, "What the heck have I done?" There were fifteen pairs in each box, accompanied by a bill for almost a thousand dollars!

Obviously, he had clicked on thirty pairs of pants

instead of the quantity of three that he wanted. (He never even noticed the massive amount of the bill.)

There's no question that people with Alzheimer's Disease will eventually develop a problem regarding dealing with their daily finances. I recall that in my father's case his lack of financial responsibility was the first sign to me that something was very, very wrong.

Throughout my growing up years it had always amazed me how he never needed to use a calculator. He could do complex math equations in his head like a bona fide mathematician. But suddenly I began to notice that he couldn't even balance his checkbook correctly.

Complications in money management are a common early sign of dementia. Trouble counting change, stacks of unopened bills or excessive purchases on credit card statements can tell the tale. Unfortunately, this may not be noticed until there is a large amount of debt already accumulated.

Sadly, there are thousands of deceitful people just waiting for the chance to take advantage of those who are memory-impaired. Telemarketers, charity scams, health care scams, and even door-to-door solicitors can be absolutely brutal to anyone who becomes an easy prey.

Try switching their regular credit cards with prepaid ones and only let them carry around small amounts of cash. With my father, I always tried to make sure he had some money in his pocket; this way it kept him feeling as if he still had some kind of independence. (Although he was always trying to pay someone for their services, even if he didn't owe them a penny.)

We must be ever diligent when seeking to protect our loved ones who are afflicted with this devastating disease. There truly are vultures perched on every corner just waiting for the right moment to swoop in!

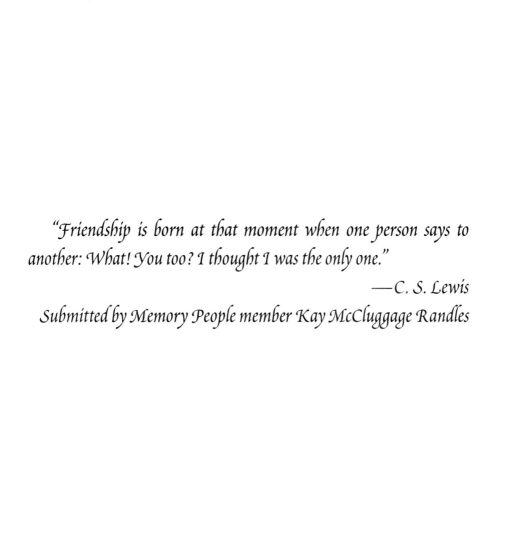

"Friendship is born at that moment when one person says to another: What! You too? I thought I was the only one."

—C. S. Lewis

Submitted by Memory People member Kay McCluggage Randles

Chapter 24

Watching Television

Whether it's *24,* starring Kiefer Sutherland or the reality show *Survivor,* the television shows that Rick and Phyllis June have always enjoyed watching together have become too difficult for Rick to follow. They now find it necessary to digitally video record (DVR) all the shows in advance. They haven't watched anything live together for quite a while now. The DVR is of great value as Rick is able to pause the program at any time and ask Phyllis June, "What is happening now? Who's that guy?" etc. Patiently, she reminds him of the plot of the show. He still enjoys watching the news. This he can handle because the stories are short, usually no longer than five minutes. Truthfully, watching television doesn't really matter to him anymore. He's just happy they're spending time sitting together.

Memory exercises and cognitive workouts are essential. I believe in that old saying, "use it or lose it," so do your best to keep loved ones' minds and hands occupied. This practice will benefit both patients and caregivers, creating a few moments of peace.

One tool that I used, which was right at my fingertips, was the boob tube. Up until the last stage of my father's battle with this disease I kept our television tuned on the *Game Show Channel* during the day. It didn't matter how old the reruns were (they could be giving away the grand prize of a 1990 Oldsmobile) it made no difference to him. As long as a constant assortment of questions flowed through the air, his mind was kept active searching for answers.

I recall him sitting at our kitchen table with *Jeopardy* pulsating in the background, when suddenly I would hear him shout out what he believed to be the correct answer! Whether he was right or wrong isn't the point. The fact that he was stimulating a few brain cells was what mattered.

After our dinner hour, my father did very well watching baseball. We rarely missed a local night game. These sporting events had conveniently taken the place of the intense mystery shows he so much used to love. The *Who done it* mysteries had simply become too much for him to manage. After a commercial interruption he would forever lose track of who murdered whom. At least with televised baseball there was always a perpetual scoreboard banner across the top of the screen.

I deeply miss watching the games with him. It's not the same without him.

I have a cute story, this happened about eight years ago. Each day we would drive our grandchildren to school.

One morning our eight-year-old grandson came down the steps and went right over to his Pop Pop and sat on his lap and gave him a big hug and kiss.

I said to him "Why don't you do that to me?" His reply was you don't have dementia. What a sweet grandson.

Written by Memory People member Lenore Smith Dickinson

Chapter 25

The Kids

The Phelps family has always been close-knit, taking vacations with their grandchildren and nieces, often camping together on the weekends. Since Rick's diagnosis, however, his concerns about making serious mistakes while caring for the younger grandkids have altered travel plans, keeping them to a minimum.

Rick and Phyllis June have four grandchildren, Shiana, Cassidi, Cortney and Brendan ranging from the ages of four to fifteen. They also have two nieces, Paige and Jade ages fifteen and thirteen.

While taking care of the two younger grandkids and attempting to cook them meals, Rick has forgotten and left the burner on the stove top turned on during three separate occasions.

Privately, with Phyllis June, he has discussed his worry about caring for them . "As much as I love having them with me, I don't think I should be left alone with them anymore. What if I make a serious mistake and one of them gets hurt? I'd never be able to forgive myself." After much discussion they decided that Rick should, indeed, no longer have the little ones by himself, unless one of the older grandchildren is there to help him out.

The youngest two, ages four and five, do not yet understand what is happening to their grandfather. The four older ones have been sat down and told flat out about Rick's Early-Onset Alzheimer's Disease. They are trying to comprehend that he's memory impaired and that gradually it's only going to get worse. The adults, however, did not go into the details with them about it being fatal.

With maturity beyond their years, the kids have stepped up to the plate and become terrific at helping Rick out, paying close attention to details and making sure everyone is safe. They have learned the necessity of reminding him of anything important, sometimes by texting him a phone message. This method seems to work better for him as it is easy for Rick to forget verbal reminders.

Now that they understand what is going on, they all seem to want to spend more time with their grandfather and uncle, which Rick absolutely adores. He too wants to spend as much time with them as possible "while he still can" remember who they are. He knows it's inevitable; a day is coming that he is severely frightened of.

Not too long ago their youngest granddaughter stayed overnight with Rick and Phyllis June. In the morning Phyllis June left for work, leaving Rick with their granddaughter. When the little girl awoke, she asked Rick if they could go to one of her favorite places for breakfast, "McDonalds," of course. He agreed and asked her if she needed help brushing her teeth and getting ready. She happily declined, claiming she was a big enough girl to handle the chore, skipping off to the bathroom. She returned shortly saying that she was ready to go, holding her little red suitcase in her hand, sandals on her feet.

Rick drove them to breakfast and let her play in the McDonald's playroom for about an hour, taking pictures of her with his camera.

Afterward, he decided to take her to her favorite local park, knowing he still had some time to kill before going to the middle school for his other granddaughter's awards ceremony.

Once at the school, while sitting in the bleachers and waiting for the ceremony to begin, he and his little granddaughter started to notice that some of the teachers were staring at them. He didn't think too much about it until he saw his adult daughter Tia walking toward them with a concerned look upon her face. "Dad, what's going on? Why is she still in her pajamas?"

This is something that the family can look back upon and laugh about now. No harm was done, but it was quite a shock at the time. This event added to Rick's concerns about watching over the grandchildren alone.

If you, the reader, are involved in caregiving or are the victim of this disease yourself, explain to all of your children exactly what's going on with you or your loved one. Children are quite keen on what is happening around them. Withholding information in an attempt to shield them from confusion or pain will ultimately make the situation worse. Assure them that this disease is not contagious. Express that there will be plenty of unfamiliar behavior and changes coming from the afflicted one and that they shouldn't be alarmed.

Children tend to be flexible and will usually bounce back quickly from the strong emotions that will constantly be surrounding them while living with an Alzheimer's patient.

If we're talking about grandparents, prepare the kids ahead of time that, with Alzheimer's, Grandma or Grandpa will eventually forget their names and even who they are.

Consider arranging a meeting with the children's school. Talk to their teachers and counselors, explaining the circumstances at home and that they should expect the kids' behavior to become noticeably different at school.

Sadly, my father had absolutely no recognition of any of his grandchildren or great-grandchildren during the last few years of his life.

This is one more in a long line of tragedies that this disease brings forth to families.

"Rick Phelps, like my father, Lester Potts, is a hero, a torch-bearer, a champion in humanity's fight against Alzheimer's disease. Rick teaches us that Alzheimer's is no match when standing toe to toe with the indomitable human spirit, which still creates, and laughs, and sings, and loves, and lives life to the fullest extent possible. In this fight, Rick is winning. And he is fighting for us as well, all of us who are personally touched by this disease. Let us learn from his experience, be inspired by his courage, and help to carry the banner of his story to others."

Written by Memory People member Daniel C. Potts, MD

Chapter 26

Rick's Daughter, Tia

My name is Tia Bookless, and Rick is my father. This is my part of the story.

It's April 22, 2010, my mother's birthday. I just called my father to see what he had gotten my mom for a gift. I was shocked to find out he had forgotten her birthday. I chalked it up to him being busy and working a lot. He has always been a "wait to the last minute shopper."

On June 30, 2010, life as I knew it changed forever.

Mom and Dad went to Newark for a neurologist appointment. My dad had been having some memory issues. The possibility of Alzheimer's had entered my mind, but I had quickly pushed that thought to the back. "He is too young!"

By midafternoon I had not yet received a phone call from them. I couldn't wait any longer, so I called my mother. Her voice sounded weak and not very happy. She told me it was Alzheimer's. All I could think of was, "This can't be happening, not to my dad. He's still in his fifties and so smart, always full of ideas. He's nothing like the people I've experienced while working in a nursing home. This terrible diagnosis cannot be right." I got off the phone and walked outside. I couldn't stop the tears from flowing.

My husband, Brian, reminded me how strong a person Dad is and how he always finds light in the worst of any situation. I kept telling myself that I must remain strong for my parents and my children.

The next step was to tell my kids. How would they take the news? They spent so much time with their grandparents. Are they going to understand? Needless to say, this was heartbreaking for them. Shiana and Cassidi, ages fifteen and twelve, knew of the disease, but not the terrible way it progresses. Cortney, age five, did not truly understand anything is wrong. Many tears were shed along with a lot of praying. We all hoped for a different diagnosis, that the doctors must have missed something.

Today, we all deal with it one day at a time. Dad is no longer able to keep the kids like he used to. He can't go to Cassidi's basketball games because the crowd and noise is too much for him. He doesn't take them out of town anymore by himself. They used to get the kids once a week, but sometimes he just isn't feeling well enough due to the disease, medicine, and stress. These are just a few of the changes in our life.

Every day I call Dad to make sure he is doing well and to see if he needs anything. He is constantly on my mind. I try to prepare myself daily for what the future will bring. I go to monthly support group meetings and Alzheimer's seminars. I will always be by my mom and dad's side.

I know that I cannot let this crush my spirit. Dad needs

my support. As I said before, I need to stay strong. I am so proud of him and all that he has done with this dire diagnosis. He could have curled up in a ball and let it destroy him, but instead he's become an advocate. A very good one at that! He has already done so much for so many people. He is setting a very good example for his grandkids and for others. He knows he has to keep going!

It hurts me to see what he and my mom are going through. I believe everything happens for a reason. God has a plan. I just pray that His plan for Dad includes keeping him happy, healthy, and strong for as long as possible. He is such a good person, and the longer he can advocate, the better. We spend as much time with him as possible. We want him to enjoy life as much as he can, while he still can. This disease has become a part of our life now, and I curse at it daily. All I can say is, "Dad, I love you dearly, and I will always be here to hold your hand. You are never alone." God Bless.

Donated by Kelsey Nielsen

Chapter 27

A Difficult Cross to Bear

When Rick began to recognize that he could no longer recall the date of his daughter Jodi's tragic death, he came to the undeniable conclusion that his memory was slipping. (This was years before his diagnosis of Early-Onset Alzheimer's.)

He believed this was unacceptable for a loving parent such as himself, so he attempted to rectify the problem by having a tattoo, dedicated to his daughter including the date of her passing, placed on his forearm.

The artwork of the tattoo is of a wooden cross that has angel wings attached to the back and a yellow ribbon spiraling down the vertical beam. Where the cross intersects the ribbon it reads, "Jodi." Further down on the ribbon is the date of her death.

Months went by before Rick finally told his wife, or anyone else for that matter, the actual reason he had the tattoo inked onto his arm.

He felt a parent should never forget such a tragic day. He

knew from experience that the hardest thing anyone ever has to do is bury a child, but not being able to remember when it happened devastated him. He could remember details of the day itself like it was yesterday, but if someone asked when it had happened he would ramble off a guess, at best. Rick kept thinking, "What kind of father would do this," not realizing the severity of his memory loss at that time.

Jodi passed away on August 21, 1997, at the tender age of twenty-two. She left behind a husband and two small toddlers, one the age of two and the other not even a year old.

Now Rick proudly wears this precious cross as it serves two special purposes: one for "remembrance" and the other for "remembering." What makes it even more precious is that his son, Eric, was the tattoo artist that designed and did the work.

"You must be willing to give up the life you had planned in order to have the life that is waiting for you."

—Joseph Campbell

Submitted by Memory People member Gary Joseph LeBlanc

Chapter 28

Saturday's Woes

Every Saturday morning Rick starts another twenty-four-hour shift of trying to stay out of trouble, while Phyllis June leaves to start her 'round-the-clock job of running an EMS squad.

For her, the job is so very rewarding. She's great with people and has the opportunity to save lives, but for Rick those twenty-four hours can feel like a month. He doesn't go anywhere, fearing something bad might happen. Instead he does simple chores around the house, nothing that would get him into too much mischief: things like running the sweeper, making the bed, etc. By 10:00 a.m. he puts on the news, not really to watch it, but just to go through the motions.

He used to love watching football on Saturday afternoons, especially Ohio State. Now that has just become one more thing he has crossed off his "don't bother" list.

By noon the feelings of isolation and boredom start

surrounding him. He almost automatically begins to search for something to do.

He never intentionally means to do anything wrong, but it seems that the laws of physics are stacked up against him.

There's a faucet in his garage that has a small leak. It has this magnetic pull summoning him to come fix it. He has fought off the urge to the point where he has hung a large sign above it saying "DON'T EVEN THINK ABOUT IT!"

When you have this disease, you live in the fear of constantly doing something wrong. The average person thinks staying out of trouble is an easy task, but for Rick it's nearly impossible. I'm not talking about anything drastic, although you never know. It's usually those little simple projects that start spiraling out of control.

Rick says it's like having a loyal pet that's so well behaved you never have to worry about them doing anything out of line. Then the day comes when you have to leave for an unusually long length of time. When you get home there are reams of toilet paper spread from one end of your house to the other.

Rick's long Saturdays aren't that good to him, but then his Sundays through Fridays aren't that great either.

Once again this shows how this disease will take a strong person and tear them down.

For now I think Rick is keeping the Post-it Note company in business.

"I used to have a handle on life . . . but then, it fell off."

—Unknown Author

Submitted by Memory People member Marsha Lynn Gomez

Chapter 29

Power Tool Ban

One afternoon Rick was scheduled to pick up his fifteen-year-old niece, Paige, from volleyball practice. As they drove home together he informed her that they were going to spend part of the evening working on a special project. Paige instantly replied, "Does Aunt Phyllis know about this?" Rick told her "No. It's going to be a surprise." Skeptical, she reminded and warned him that her aunt absolutely hated surprises. Rick told her, "Trust me . . . This one is a good one, I promise."

Previously, Rick had purchased a mounting bracket for the flat-screen television in his and Phyllis June's bedroom. Up until now the TV was sitting precariously on top of a dresser, taking up valuable space. Now he had other plans.

When they got back to the house, Rick and Paige removed the television from the dresser and pulled the dresser away from the now-exposed wall. Rick held the bracket up to where he believed would be the best viewing spot from the bed. Using a pencil he traced the frame of the bracket on the wall and marked where the screw holes should go. Then he grabbed his cordless drill. Paige was alarmed at the sight of it, asking with great concern, "Are you sure about this, Uncle Ricky?" He responded proudly, "Are you kidding? She's going to love this."

With decades of experience under his belt, Rick drilled the four holes necessary and inserted the plastic anchors for the screws. He fastened the bracket to the wall and asked Paige to screw the mount into the back of the 32" flat screen while he held it up.

Paige got the first screw in and Rick told her to hurry with the next one as the television was getting heavy. After she tightened the second screw, Rick yelled that he had to let go. Everything came crashing down! Paige grabbed a corner of the television and, between the two of them, they prevented it from smashing to the floor. Out of breath and staring at each other, they slowly looked up and saw a five-inch gaping hole ripped out of the wall. The missing piece of drywall was still bolted to the television!

It had not registered with Rick that at least one of the mount screws needed to be tightened securely into a stud inside the wall.

"Aunt Phyllis is going to kill us!" Paige fretted. He tried to reassure her that everything was going to be fine.

After cleaning up the mess Rick told Paige, "Watch this." He grabbed a large oval mirror and hung it right over the giant abyss that he had created.

(He silently spent the rest of the night praying that Phyllis June would never find the hole until long after he was gone.)

The next morning she returned from her night shift.

The first thing she noticed was Rick sitting quietly at the kitchen table, drinking a cup of coffee. (He has never been good at lying or even keeping a secret.) She took one look at him and asked demandingly, "What did you do?" "Nothing," he told her. She shook her head and said, "Don't give me that; what happened?" After a couple of seconds in deep thought he responded, "Now, don't panic, it's really not that bad." Timidly, he brought her into the bedroom, removed the mirror, and showed her his new handiwork.

From that point on Rick has not been allowed to use any power tools or anything else that even resembles something that runs on electricity, without adult supervision.

As far as Paige goes, she was absolutely right from the very beginning: Aunt Phyllis doesn't like surprises.

The point of this story is that, four or five years ago, Rick would never have attempted this project without first securing the bracket into a wall stud. He would've known better.

Tragically, Alzheimer's disease has stolen his ability to make proper decisions, which is one of the reasons that those suffering from this disease desperately need family members and caregivers to help direct them through this campaign.

"Kind words can be short and easy to speak, but their echoes are truly endless.

—Mother Teresa
Submitted by Florida M. LeBlanc

Chapter 30

Cold Feet Leads to Cold Shoulders

Not long ago Rick and Phyllis June sat down to discuss the possibility of removing the carpet in their front room and hallway and then having it replaced, sometime in the future, with hardwood floors.

"Future" is the key word here. When dealing with the disease of Alzheimer's, the loss of a sense of time doesn't only relate to the past or present, it also deals heavily with the inability to comprehend the time that lies ahead.

When the day arrived for Rick to begin this project, he first needed to pick up his niece, Paige, from volleyball practice. As she slid into the passenger side of the front seat, he asked her for her help in undertaking this job. She rolled her eyes and asked skeptically, "Are you sure about this, Uncle Ricky?" Rick assured her that he and Aunt Phyllis June had already decided on the matter.

When they got to the house, they started moving the furniture around. Rick gathered all the tools he needed: a hammer, pliers, and a utility knife. (You may have noticed that none of these tools have an electrical cord.)

They started pulling up the carpet. When they got a large-enough section lifted, Rick cut it and carried it out to the garage.

The project took them about four hours. He then began sweeping the floor. He noticed some tacks exposed so he picked up a tack hammer and repaired them.

Rick was feeling a sense of pride, thinking this was a win-win situation. Everything would be ready for the delivery of the floor layers and, this way, they would save some money on the labor.

After standing back and taking a good look at his handiwork, he had to admit the place looked kind of rough with the subfloor being au naturel. Nevertheless, he was pleased enough to head off to bed with a smile on his face.

Phyllis June got home around 8:30 the next morning after working a twenty-four-hour shift. Rick greeted her outside and helped her grab her gear out of the car. As they were walking into the house, he happily told her he had a surprise for her inside. With trepidation, Phyllis June's eyes probably rolled around even more than that of their niece!

Entering the house, she only had to take a couple of steps before it became obvious what the grand surprise was. She quickly turned to him and, with shock, got the words out, "What on earth did you do?" Rick immediately knew that maybe his surprise wasn't so grand after all.

He told her that he and Paige had ripped the carpet out. "I can see that! Why would you do such a thing?" The tension in the air could be cut with a knife. He replied,

"So we can put down the hardwood floors. This will save us some money."

As she drew in a deep breath and slowly exhaled, Phyllis June was able to release some of the adrenaline built up in her system, then she spoke. "Rick. I know you mean well, but we're not getting new floors tomorrow or even next week, probably not for many months to come. You need to think these things through." "I thought I did," he told her.

Not only does this disease affects one's sense of time, it also affects the ability to make proper decisions.

For the next four months, Phyllis June tried to never look down while walking through her house.

To this day Rick says, "It's a good thing she loves me."

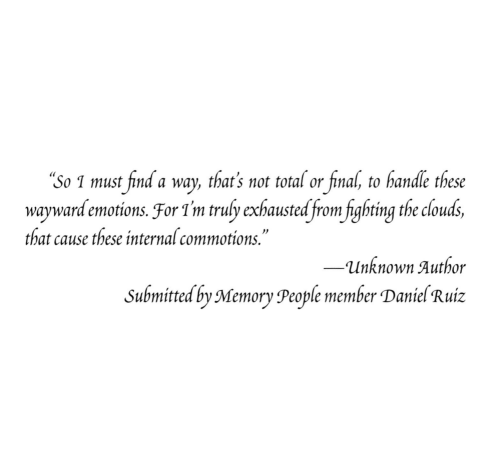

"So I must find a way, that's not total or final, to handle these wayward emotions. For I'm truly exhausted from fighting the clouds, that cause these internal commotions."

—Unknown Author
Submitted by Memory People member Daniel Ruiz

Chapter 31

The Camper

Hearkening back to the early years of his life, Rick recalls, with fondness, the way his entire family enjoyed camping. They owned an Apache pop-up trailer and often used it for getaways along the Lake Erie side of Ohio.

After he married Phyllis June they would borrow her sister's camper for their own getaway weekends, or longer, if they could. Ultimately, they purchased their own trailer and found a beautiful piece of land to park it on about fifteen miles from their house. This location was close enough that they could spend the night and still make it to work easily in the morning without having to leave at some ridiculous hour.

Through the years, the tranquility of this place has given Rick exactly what the doctors and everybody else tell him that he needs: "A stress-free environment."

The place has all the comforts of home, including both running water and electricity. It's a place where he can just slow down, kick back, and try to put his worries out of his racing mind.

Phyllis June has had her concerns about him being there alone. What if something happens or he loses his cell phone and she can't reach him? Nevertheless, he seemed to handle it well during the early stage of his disease. She reminds herself that he has had their dogs for company, and she truly is not far away.

Their weekends aren't always spent alone. Sometimes they invite family and friends over for cookouts, and the crowds don't bother Rick like they tend to at home. Being outdoors is perfect since there aren't any walls for the voices to bounce off like back at the house.

This upcoming spring Rick is hoping to use the trailer as much as possible. He wisely plans to "play it by ear."

A few problems do occasionally pop up; for instance, remembering what to bring with him, including the keys, to the camper. And on one trip he brought the dogs and forgot the dog food! He finds himself having to call Phyllis June, asking her to bring things he forgets.

For the time being, the place serves him well, but once again I want you, the reader, to realize that all people with Alzheimer's respond differently. Taking your loved one out of his or her routine environment can intensify their confusion immensely.

"The people who are hardest to love, are usually the ones who need it the most."

—Unknown Author
Submitted by Memory people member Tina Gatson

Chapter 32

When Repairmen Come to the House

Rick and Phyllis June decided to have satellite TV installed in their camper. Before the scheduled serviceman came to the house to install the equipment, Phyllis June informed them, in advance, that Rick would be there, but to be advised that he suffers from memory impairment. Like everything else when dealing with large companies, the message got lost in the shuffle of paperwork.

When the installer finally showed up, he spent about half an hour working on the installation before he realized that the external junction box for the cable on the camper wasn't properly working. Rick suggested running the cable through the floors. The serviceman agreed but told Rick he would have to come back another day because this would take a different work order. Rick replied, "You got to be kidding me? You're right here, right now, standing in my driveway and you're going to have to come back because you need a separate piece of paper in order to drill a hole into my floor!"

Rick then insisted that he call his supervisor; he wanted to talk to him or her right away. After talking to that supervisor, Rick demanded to talk with *her* supervisor.

To make a short story even shorter, they gave the serviceman permission to finish the job right then and there.

What these service companies do not realize is that although Rick handled himself very well, the aftereffects could drag on for days.

Here's another quick example of a similar dilemma. Rick changed Internet services, and the new provider turned out to be nothing but a problem. He kept getting knocked off-line two to three times an hour. When he called up to complain, the company decided it would be best to send out a technician. The guy came out to the house and figured it would be best to just leave Rick with a new modem box to hook up by himself. He didn't argue with him because he thought it be best if the serviceman just left.

A year ago Rick would have hooked up that box without even reading the directions. Now it was as if he was trying to install an octopus to the computer with all the wires and cables.

He called the Internet provider back and told them to cancel his subscription and that he was mailing them back their modem.

Anytime there's a service call that comes out to the house, Rick's anxiety climbs through the roof.

Telemarketers calling or salesmen banging on the door are just two of the reasons that Rick no longer answers the telephone or the front door unless he knows who it is.

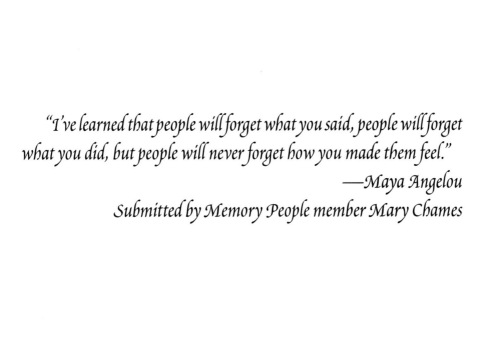

"I've learned that people will forget what you said, people will forget what you did, but people will never forget how you made them feel."

—Maya Angelou

Submitted by Memory People member Mary Chames

Chapter 33

Mr. Phelps Goes to Washington

In May of 2010, Rick and Phyllis June, along with six hundred other Alzheimer's patients and advocates, were honored to be invited by the Alzheimer's Association to speak with U.S. Senators and Congressmen in Washington, D.C.

On their first night in the city they were scheduled to go to a conference where there would be several guest speakers, including former Speaker of the House Newt Gingrich, whose sister-in-law suffers from Alzheimer's.

Prior to Mr. Gingrich taking the podium, it was announced that he would not be accepting any political questions. The format must stay on the topic of Alzheimer's.

He spoke for a little more than twenty minutes. When he was finished it appeared to Rick that Mr. Gingrich was leaving for the evening. Rick told Phyllis June that he'd be right back and excused himself from the table. Hurrying outside, he found Mr. Gingrich conducting an interview for a television newscast. Rick waited patiently, then walked up to where the security guards were standing. He leaned into the group and bravely asked the former Speaker if he could have a word with him. Gingrich politely gave his consent and the guards let Rick approach him. He asked Rick what was on his mind. Rick explained that he had been diagnosed with the disease and how he was truly concerned that this group of 600 people had come from all over the country to speak to their Senators and Congressmen tomorrow and that most of these public servants weren't even here in the city! Gingrich assured him, "You shouldn't worry about that too much. The representatives working for them probably know more about the subject than they actually do. They will relay the message the way it should be told. Tell them what you believe they need to hear." Rick agreed to do as he was told, but still feared that their message would never really be heard.

Then Rick asked the former Speaker if he would be willing to pose with him for a picture. Mr. Gingrich said he'd be honored and Rick put one of the bodyguards to work.

When he got back to the table Phyllis June asked him, "Where the heck have you been?" He answered gallantly, "I ran down Newt Gingrich, and we chitchatted for a while." She stared at him in disbelief and replied, "Right! So really, where were you?" Rick smiled and proudly pulled out his iPhone, showing her three pictures of himself shaking hands with former Speaker of the House, Newt Gingrich.

"My friends, love is better than anger. Hope is better than fear. Optimism is better than despair. So let's be loving, hopeful, and optimistic. And we can change the world."

—Jack Layton

Submitted by Memory People member Kim Leslie

Chapter 34

Washington, D.C., Day Two

The next day the whole group went to the U.S. Senate building. They broke off into groups of ten and were assigned different senators' offices to visit. The building was nothing shy of being impressive, plush all the way.

Rick's fear of the senators being absent was right on track. They did, however, have someone there to represent them. The small group sat around a long table in a conference room. The young advocate from the Alzheimer's Association introduced everyone in her group by name to the senators' aids. The representative asked if anybody wanted to start off by saying anything. Nobody spoke up, so Rick took the opportunity to jump right in.

Addressing the representative he explained that, at the age of fifty-seven, he had been diagnosed with Early-Onset Alzheimer's. Holding her business card in his hand he said to her, "I'm so glad I have this card because it's the only way I'll ever be able to recall your name. I truly hope you will remember mine, and everyone else's here in the group, after this meeting is finished."

He went on to describe the daily symptoms those suffering from the disease endure. He also told her the fact that, currently, every sixty-eight seconds someone is being diagnosed with Alzheimer's disease. If a cure or a newly discovered method to slow this disease down isn't discovered soon, it will surely bankrupt the health care system of our nation. Alzheimer's alone will cost Medicare and Medicaid twenty trillion dollars annually by the year 2050. Funding the research of this disease should be looked at as an investment for our country's future.

All in all, Rick is glad he made the trip. Traveling with this disease is very difficult. He's not exactly sure what really got accomplished, but he felt it was an honor to be there.

The following month they were invited to the state capital building in Columbus, Ohio, to speak with state representatives. Once again there was a large group of people all sitting in a roomy atrium waiting for the event to begin. Suddenly, there was an announcement that there would be a slight change of plans. None of the senators or congressmen were going to be there! Apparently on Thursdays none of them are in the building.

Rick could hardly believe what he was hearing. How could they plan an event like this on a day that they're never even here!

Ohio Governor John Kasich did speak to the crowd, however. He seems to be one who truly understands the situation. He has a best friend whose wife was diagnosed with Alzheimer's. He has a feel for what the family and caregivers actually go through. He also understands the importance of financial funding to find a cure.

Many of the people who went to this event gave up a day's pay in hopes that their being there would make a difference. You would think these government officials would have at least made an attempt to show up!

"Stand up when others choose to sit down; Step forward when others prefer to step back; Speak out when the voices of silence are so deafening."

—Unknown Author

Submitted by Rick Phelps, Founder of Memory People

Chapter 35

The Elephant in the Room

There are two words that should never appear in the same sentence together: embarrassment and dementia.

When Rick was first diagnosed with Early-Onset Alzheimer's, he told everyone he had the disease. He had the mind-set that assumed everyone was going to notice his dementia anyway. Now that he has met and talked with so many people that have the same disease, he realizes how such a large percentage of them do not want to discuss their illness with anyone. Alzheimer's or any other kind of dementia is nothing to be ashamed of. Being memory impaired is a disability, and the general public needs to be educated on this. For years this disease has been put on the back burner because of embarrassment and denial. We would truly be further ahead of today's research if it weren't for such acts. President Ronald Reagan could have kept his diagnosis private, but instead he courageously wrote a letter to the nation sharing honestly his diagnosis.

This started us out on the march to fight this disease that we are currently on.

This disease seems to be like an elephant in the room; some people think if they don't talk about it, it will just go away. Well, it doesn't go away, it only gets worse.

Talk with your family and friends about this disease. Educate them. Knowledge is power. Hiding behind this disease won't do you or your family any good. Spreading awareness will help everyone.

You are right where you should be at this moment. Now it is time to move on to what is next. Whether your life up to this point has been easy or whether it has been difficult, you are here just the same. And your destiny does not care about your past. There are plenty of reasons why you find yourself here at this time.

What matters much more, though, are the reasons you now have for moving forward.

As good as they have been, your triumphs of your past are now little more than pleasant memories. As painful as they once were, past failures are now behind you.

Written by Memory People member Kaye Lynn Hardesty Andrews

Chapter 36

Memory People Begins

After being diagnosed, Rick started searching the Internet for any information he could find about Early-Onset Alzheimer's.

He found a site that had many chat rooms on this subject. He posted a question and waited, and waited. Finally, late that evening, someone responded. He posted another query and didn't get a response this time until late the next afternoon. "This is insane," he said to himself. Someone with this disease shouldn't have to wait like this. By the time they eventually have an answer they'll never remember what the question originally was. This to him was completely unacceptable.

Rick had been a member of Facebook for quite some time now, so he decided to start a group on there, specifically for Alzheimer's and dementia-related patients and caregivers. It was very important to Rick to have this combination because he knew this would create the perfect opportunity for them to learn from each other.

Thanksgiving Day, November 24, 2010, he founded the group Memory People. The only problem now was that Rick was the only member.

He went into other Alzheimer's chat rooms and started mentioning his group and inviting others to join. People started to respond asking what the group was about and who's there. Rick explained that his goal was to bring awareness and have a place for support where people didn't have to wait a whole day or more to find answers to problems. As for who is there, well, ME!

Before long he had twenty members, and it started growing rapidly. It's important that I explain to you, the reader, that this is not an ordinary Facebook group. This isn't a place where you post what you had for dinner or what you saw at the movies. Everything must stay on the topic of Alzheimer's or other dementia-related diseases and support. It is a closed site. You have to be a member and what is posted can only be viewed by other members. What is written there stays there.

Within a couple of months, Rick had over three hundred members that had joined. Everyone was astonished at the amount of information that was available and how quickly it could be retrieved.

He soon began receiving thank you messages for all the support that members were getting. He explained that it wasn't due to him; it was coming from *everyone* in the group. When someone posted a question about a problem they were facing, solutions would come flying in almost immediately.

It got to the point where Rick had to enlist some administrators to help him with the group. Keep in mind that Rick is memory impaired himself. This became a lot for him to handle. Fortunately, he found a few special volunteers to help monitor the site to make sure everyone was staying on topic and to help enroll new members. (If people stray off subject, it's not the end of the world; after all many of the members are suffering from dementia.)

"*Never doubt that a small group of thoughtful, committed citizens can change the world, it is the only thing that ever has.*"

—*Margaret Mead*

Submitted by Memory People member Leeanne Chames

Chapter 37

The Balloon Launch

Reaching the two-hundred-Memory-People-member mark *so quickly* truly surprised Rick and his fellow Memory People administrators. They decided to do something special that all the members could take part in, so as to celebrate this milestone.

(I want to point out that it's not the amount of new members that's significant, it's the amount of support and awareness that was brought forward.)

Waiting patiently, Rick dearly wanted Phyllis June to become the 200th member. As the numbers continued to grow, he watched closely and let her know exactly when to join.

After tossing around several ideas, it was decided that a balloon launch would be just the thing to do to commemorate this exciting progress. Since the current members were scattered across the globe, living in so many different time zones, it was decided that Rick would just choose the day and leave the time of the launch up to each individual. At this time there were already members living in the United Kingdom, Europe, Canada, Australia, and the United States.

Then they came up with the idea of attaching a note to everyone's balloon in order to introduce whoever discovered it to Memory People and its goals. They also posted the message on the website so everyone could just easily print it. This is the message that floated across international skies:

> *"This Balloon is a Symbol of Awareness for Alzheimer's Disease and comes in the form of a 'Hello' From Memory People"*
>
> *Memory People was created by Rick Phelps. He felt a strong need for "Real-Time" communication when having a question regarding Alzheimer's disease. Rick himself has Early Onset Alzheimer's Disease. The mission of Memory People is to bring people diagnosed with Alzheimer's and their Caregivers together around the world to support one another in a private and secure fashion which is respectful to all involved.*
>
> *Rick said, "When someone has a question about Alzheimer's disease, I want them to have the option of not only getting an answer, but actually forming a relationship with that person." Thus, Memory People was born.*
>
> *Some say Memory People is like a family, with all the dynamics of love and compassion, mixed with anger and pain as this disease dances with our emotions and our lives. We work together as one to find answers, to build a community, and to*

give support to one another through the turbulent times of illness, aging, and memory loss. We offer support and information to one another in a safe, private, and respectful setting.

If you have been touched by Alzheimer's disease, or know someone that has, we would love you to join our family it's FREE! Help Us Raise Awareness for Alzheimer's Disease.

Rick had one problem with releasing his message into the sky; he has a terrible fear of balloons, he always has.

I have now recently found out, since writing this book, that there is an actual term for such a fear; it's called "Globophobia."

The release was set for Sunday, February 4, 2011, so Rick went out the Friday afternoon prior, to a local Hallmark gift shop and purchased three "intimidating" balloons. He asked if they could place them in a large plastic bag for him so they wouldn't be attacking him from behind while driving. He took a picture of them with his I-Phone in the back of his Jeep and drove home. He parked his vehicle in the garage and left the driver's side window halfway down. Since it was February and they kept their cats' litter box inside the heated garage keeping their furry friends quite cozy during the Ohio winter months, he thought nothing of the open window.

After a peaceful Friday night of staying home relaxing and getting excited about Sunday's event, Rick walked in to the garage Saturday morning and no longer saw the balloons floating in the back of the Jeep. He stepped closer and looked inside, spying the empty plastic bag on the floor and what was left of his Zeppelins scattered everywhere.

These weren't your average large-sized balloons; they were promised to reach the mile-high mark.

While Rick and Phyllis June were having a quiet Friday night, their two cats were having a party in the garage—a gathering that I'm sure they dreamt about for many catnaps to come!

Rick found himself back at the gift store buying three more of those dreadful floating devices.

Finally they met Tia, Brian, and the girls at the fairgrounds to "set his fears free." Brian recorded the event, and they all had a moment of silence for all those who have lost their battle against Alzheimer's.

The next launch is set for the two-thousand-member mark, which I believe will be met by the time this book reaches your hands.

"Memory People is more than support. It is a growing movement of the most generous, wonderful people with first hand knowledge of what it's like to live with or care for the many types of dementia. Every story is different, but there are common threads. These threads have woven the most beautiful fabric. We feel connected and strong. And never alone."

Written by Memory People member Ruthie Rosenfeld

Chapter 38

Memory People II and Spin-off Sites

Not long after creating the group, "Memory People," Rick realized that everyone who is dealing with this disease needs a diversion from it, so he decided to start a "spin-off site" called "Memory People II." This is a place where patients and caregivers can go to discuss any topic they want except Alzheimer's and any other dementia-related diseases. As Rick puts it, "Mr. Alzheimer's is not allowed here. That's what the original site is for."

He has made a ruling that almost anything goes here, especially jokes and just chattering. But no offensive or foul language or off-color subject matter. Once again, this includes Mr. "you know who!"

Memory People II has been such a huge success that it has lead to creating other spin-off sites, including even game night on Saturday evenings. This began as a "Truth or Dare" type of game where someone would post something they did in their lifetime, while others tried to figure out if it was true or false. It has worked well at breaking the ice, giving people a break from the life-consuming disease monster. The site has been such a success that it has evolved into other games and activities.

The following is a list of other sites that were created and have become extremely popular:

- Memory People Prayer Chain—a site where you can go to offer, and ask for, prayer for you or someone else.
- Memory People Recipes—where participants can exchange recipes with each other. This is another fun way to connect and get to know one another better.
- Memory People For Your Health—where readers can encourage each other and share tips on living a healthy lifestyle. Issues tackled may include: weight loss, nutrition, exercise, etc.
- Memory People Tunes—posting of songs for everyone to enjoy.
- Memory People Broad Squad—especially meant for women, this one keeps the discussion on the topic of Alzheimer's but realizes that there may be some things that the women aren't comfortable posting on the main Memory People site.
- Memory People Suggestions—the posting of input but with a catch . . . if you have an idea, or suggestion, share it along with a solution and please post it. Your input is important.
- Memory People Memorial—a place for the those who have already joined Memory People to remember their loved ones that they have lost to Alzheimer's,

and any other dementia-related diseases, and to honor any fallen members.

- Memory People Resources—a site to share helpful resources already found in this journey of memory impairment.
- Memory People Crafters—a place to share the latest projects and get great ideas for all kinds of crafts, woodwork, paint, sewing, etc.

These spin-off sites are another example of how Memory People has grown and moved forward at amazing speed since Rick founded the group.

Members have a special bond with another.

Enormous support!

Many memories are being shared.

Opportunity to the change people's lives.

Reaching out to others.

Yearning for there to be a cure for all memory impairments.

People who understand what you're going through.

Effective in raising awareness of memory impairments.

Offering support & love for each other.

Patients, caregivers, advocates supporting each other.

Learning from each other.

Enable people to share their stories without judgement.

Written by Memory People member

Cheryl Stevenson Kearney

Chapter 39

Rick's Personal Assistant, Leeanne Chames

My mother-in-law was diagnosed with Alzheimer's in January of 2010. At that time, I didn't know much about the disease, other than seeing what it was doing to her. I was concerned by her repetition and not seeming to be able to remember things that she always had known. I started researching the Internet like crazy, so I could help my husband help his parents. We all saw something was going on, and one day my husband mentioned it to his dad. There was almost relief that he wasn't alone in this, that we were all going to help figure this out and get Mom some help.

In August, I found the discussion boards online and signed up and participated a bit. I never did really get too involved there; I'm not really sure why. I've been on forums before and become very involved.

It was early January 2011 when I saw someone had left

the link to "Memory People," so I clicked on it. Someone added me to the group and literally, within seconds, I was getting welcomed right and left. There was some really heavy stuff going on, but I was only a long-distance caregiver to my mother-in-law. I said, "Thank you, but I'm not sure if I'm in the right place." Right away a fellow member messaged me, "You're in the right place." Just those words made me feel better, so I jumped right in, always making sure to welcome new members. After all, that had made a big difference for me. After a week or two I realized that I was getting close to these people. I began to wonder if I could do this. I had jumped in, all the way, and realized that people were struggling with really heart-wrenching situations. Not all of them were going to make it out alive. I'm not one to keep people away emotionally. Once I let someone in, I let them all the way into my heart. So I wrote Rick and said that I didn't feel that Memory People was for me. I wished him and the group well, but felt that I didn't belong there. Then I left the group before he could respond.

All that day I couldn't shake this feeling that I had made a huge mistake. Eventually, Rick wrote back to me and said how sorry he was that I felt that way, that he was sorry to see me go, but that he wouldn't force anyone to stay. His words meant a lot, but truthfully made me feel worse. By the next day I was a mess. I knew deep inside I had walked out of somewhere I was supposed to be, so I sent another message to Rick and asked if I could return. I didn't explain a lot, just that I realized that this is where I was supposed to be. Right away he responded and said, "Once you're a part of Memory People, you're always a part of Memory People."

Soon after that, Rick asked me if I would think about becoming an Administrator for the group. That was the first of many steps I would take in this journey with him and everyone else there. I was scared to death, but when someone else has confidence in you, it makes all the difference in the world. He said something that startled me, "This may be your calling." I wondered how he could possibly think that. He barely even knew me. The one thing I did know for sure was that God had taken my hand and walked me from my couch to my computer and said, "Leeanne, I have some work for you to do."

I threw myself into Memory People, welcoming people, crying with them, and laughing with them. At times, the heartache and tears were almost too much to bear. There were many times I had to walk away from the computer because I couldn't read the words through the tears, but I was not going to walk away from my new friends ever again.

Soon Rick started a video diary which spoke from his heart. He would describe in honest detail how he not only would forget why he went into a room, but he also wasn't able to realize what room he was even in. By far, the hardest days were when Rick would have to say he couldn't be on Memory People, that the posts weren't making any sense and he just couldn't comprehend them. How ironic. Here was this wonderful thing he created to help people, and it was being taken away from him. My heart was heavy with the knowledge that the day would come that he couldn't be on Memory People, or even remember what it was. So I messaged him and said that I knew the day would come that I would log on to Memory People and *he* wouldn't be there, but *I* would. I never wanted him to worry that I would leave again.

In late February he was scheduled to be interviewed at a local radio station. He and Phyllis June were to be on the show together, but she became ill and couldn't make it. Their daughter Tia went with Rick instead. We put out reminders on Memory People so members would listen and call in. At 9:00 a.m. (6:00 a.m. my time) the show started. The host said he would take calls, and I had promised I would call in, so with shaking hands and feeling like my heart would leap out of my chest, I dialed the phone number. I was the first caller, and I was scared to death. Another step forward. Many members of the group listened as we commented about Memory People and what it meant to us. We had a blast!

I talked with Rick for a few minutes, and after I hung up and got back on Memory People I saw that many, many members had been cheering me on the whole time.

It was a turning point for the group. It was as if Memory People was given new life that day. It wasn't just typed words on a page anymore; we were hearing each other's voices. It brought tears of joy.

Rick hit a really rough patch for a few months. This was the worst I had ever seen him in. I always wanted to know if he was having a worse day than usual, because if he was, I wouldn't try to go over questions and the things-to-do list with him. It was just too much for him. Days turned into weeks where he couldn't go over things with me. Then one day he said to me, "We knew this day would come." I hated those words. He asked me to make a post in Memory People to say that he was really slipping and just couldn't be on like he had been. I remember thinking on that day, as I composed that post for Rick, that I never hated Alzheimer's as much as I did at that moment.

Memory People continued to grow, gathering people in who were caught on this terrible journey and had little or no hope or understanding from friends and family. We continued to cry and laugh together and support each other through everything we went through.

They say there is a time and place for everything. I believe this is Rick's time. This is Rick's place. I believe that God's hand is on Rick and Phyllis June. Through them, lives have been changed, the hopeless have found hope, and hearts that were broken have begun to heal. Rick's legacy will continue, until we make Alzheimer's a memory, itself.

This chapter was graciously donated by Leeanne Chames.

"A friend is someone who knows the song in your heart and can sing it back to you when you have forgotten the words."

—Bernard Meltzer

Submitted by Memory People member Leeanne Chames

Chapter 40

A Song for Awareness

Rick has an old friend of forty-some years by the name of Dan Mitchell. They have been close friends ever since high school, hanging out and playing guitars all throughout their bright-eyed days. Soon after graduation, Dan left to follow his dream to be a musician, singer, and songwriter. He now resides in Nashville, Tennessee.

Dan's true love is writing songs. One of his most well known is, "If You're Gonna Play in Texas (You Gotta Have a Fiddle in the Band)," which the Country Band "Alabama" turned into a gold record.

Running it over and over in his mind, Rick couldn't shake the idea of contacting Dan about getting together and writing a song about this repulsive disease of Alzheimer's. When he contacted Dan, he responded that Rick must have been reading his mind, telling him that he had been thinking about doing something like this for a couple of months now.

Rick told him he wanted it titled "While I Still Can . . ."

He suggested to Dan that he should become a member of Memory People so he could read the posts and let what he learns soak in for a while. For instance, Rick was always posting that "time is my enemy." That has now become the fifth line of the song.

Together they worked on the lyrics, and finally Dan put down the music.

Dan owns a recording studio in Nashville called "The Tracking Room" where he has worked with many of the great country music artists such as: Brooks & Dunn, Reba, and Kenny Chesney, just to name a few.

Dan had several studio musicians join him in recording the first track of the song.

The following musicians have donated their time and talent to help make this song possible and a dream of Rick's come true; using music as a catalyst in spreading awareness of this terrible disease.

Buddy Hyatt: Piano, Jim Hyatt: Bass Guitar, Scott Williamson: Drums, Joel Key: Acoustic Guitar, Scotty Saunders: Steel Guitar, and Larry Franklin: Fiddle.

Back when Rick and Dan were in high school they were each dating girls which came from strong religious backgrounds. They too were best friends. The church the girls attended was having a hayride and invited Rick and Dan to come along, asking that they bring their guitars along to do a sing-along. This happened to take place during the hot, summer months of Ohio, so Rick and Dan decided to wear shorts to the event. When they arrived at the church they noticed they were receiving icy stares from everybody. Rick asked his girlfriend, "What's going on?" Embarrassed, she whispered, "I can't believe the both of you wore shorts. The church doesn't believe in such things." Amused, Rick and Dan later wrote their first song together called, "I Love my Shorts."

Dan has been a great friend to Rick, and he has told me how their relationship has brought a special meaning to his life.

When you have the chance, you really must listen to the song they created, "While I Still Can." It is absolutely beautiful and poignant, containing a strong message about the reality and heartbreak of Alzheimer's Disease.

Here are the lyrics:

While I Still Can . . .
By Dan Mitchell and Rick Phelps

. . . SOMETIMES YESTERDAY
CAN SEEM A MILLION YEARS AWAY
AND I'LL FORGET EXACTLY WHAT TO SAY
WHEN ASKED ABOUT MY PAST

TIME IS MY ENEMY
THAT'S WHY I'M LIVING FOR RIGHT NOW
TOMORROW'S JUST TOO FAR TO THINK ABOUT
MY HEART ONLY KNOWS ONE TASK

Chorus:
WHILE I STILL CAN
I'M GONNA HOLD MY BABIES TO MY CHEST
THANK GOD FOR ALL THE WAYS THAT I'VE BEEN
BLESSED
RELIVE EACH SINGLE DAY FROM BAD TO BEST

WHILE I STILL CAN
I'LL TRY TO HELP MY LOVED ONES UNDERSTAND
HOW MEMORIES CAN FLY LIKE GRAINS OF SAND
AND THAT I'LL REMEMBER THEM
WHILE I STILL CAN

DON'T ASK ME TO DECIDE
WHICH WAY I WANT MY ROAD TO TURN
MY GOD BY NOW I THOUGHT YOU WOULD HAVE LEARNED
I WILL FOLLOW YOU ON FAITH

WHEN I FALL ASLEEP
THE DARKNESS AND THE DEMONS STEAL MY DREAMS
OF HOW THINGS WERE AND HOW THEY STILL
COULD BE
IN A SWEETER PLACE

Chorus:
WHILE I STILL CAN
I'M GONNA HOLD MY BABIES TO MY BREAST
THANK GOD FOR ALL THE WAYS THAT I'VE BEEN
BLESSED
RELIVE EACH SINGLE DAY FROM BAD TO BEST

WHILE I STILL CAN
I'LL TRY TO HELP MY LOVED ONES UNDERSTAND
HOW MEMORIES CAN FLY LIKE GRAINS OF SAND
AND THAT I'LL REMEMBER THEM
WHILE I STILL CAN

Bridge:
CHOICES, DECISIONS, FRUSTRATIONS AND PAIN
KNOWING I'M GOING TO FORGET HER SOMEDAY

Chorus:
WHILE I STILL CAN
I'LL CHALLENGE ALL MY LOVED ONES, EVERY FRIEND
TO LOOK INSIDE THEIR HEARTS AND UNDERSTAND
THAT I WILL LOVE THEM
I WILL LOVE THEM
WHILE I STILL CAN

"When we help each other, everyone wins."
Written by Memory People member Alexandra Faer Bryan

Chapter 41

The Newsletter

In March of 2011, during a Saturday game night on "Memory People II," Rick and another member named Harry Urban were jokingly writing, "It sure would be nice if we had a newsletter to keep track of things around here." Then almost simultaneously they posted "Leeanne could do that!"

The next thing they knew she responded that, if this was something they sincerely wanted, she would make it happen. She enthusiastically took on the new role of being an editor.

Together they started brainstorming about what should be discussed in the newsletter and what to name it. At first, it was called "Memory People News." Then it was decided that it would be in good merriment to hold a contest between members to rename it. Linda Daniels's suggestion of "The Memory People Page" was chosen as the winner.

The monthly newsletter has now become a way for

members to read about upcoming events, speaking engagements, radio shows, or any other media involvement concerning Memory People. They also run inspirational stories of the journeys that fellow members go through during their time of caregiving or in dealing with memory impairment themselves.

When the idea of interviewing members came to light, the first person Leeanne chose to confabulate with was Guy Michetti. He has been a longtime group member and has inspired many other readers in the way that he has cared for his wife who suffers from Alzheimer's disease.

I've always said that there's something more spectacular about a story that is told by someone who is walking down the same path in the same pair of shoes as the reader.

This newsletter has become Leeanne's "baby." After going through a period of some frustration, and also feeling like maybe she could not do the project proper justice, her husband gave her a crash course in using Microsoft Word. She also got a much welcome indoctrination from Harry Urban who has worked on similar projects. He answered many of the questions that were bothering her since she took on this new position. All of this and feeding off the devoted faith that Rick and others had in her, Leeanne's work began to shine.

Every week the newsletter gets more subscribers. Members have been making extra copies and passing them out to family, friends, assisted living facilities, and doctors' offices.

It has become just one more way that Memory People has discovered that it can help spread awareness of Alzheimer's and other dementia-related diseases.

"Don't cry over the past it's gone. Don't stress over the future it hasn't arrived. Live in the present and make it beautiful."

—Unknown Author

Submitted by Memory People member Marlu Gibson

Chapter 42

The Ride Along

Not long ago Rick shared an idea with Phyllis June: he'd been thinking about signing up for what they call a "Ride Along." (This would make him an observer while riding in an ambulance out of the same station where he worked as an EMT for so many years.)

Showing her agreement, Phyllis June got a hold of the so-called "powers-that-be" and they scheduled him for a Saturday, which she works anyway. They were very glad to have him, since he had spent almost half his lifetime working with them. Most of his coworkers hadn't seen Rick since he stepped down after his diagnosis.

As the days got closer to his scheduled ride along, Rick noticed anxiety building up inside of him. When the Friday before finally arrived it was not what you would call a good day for him. He realized he may have still had some stirred-up emotions from what happened on his last run, and that was what was causing the extra nervousness.

Arriving at the squad house around 9:00 a.m., his

initial reaction was joy in seeing his old friends, especially when they began to exchange stories about past runs with him.

They decided to go and have breakfast while waiting for their first call of the day to come in. Rick sat in the back of the ambulance in what is called the "jump seat." It had been one and a half years since the last time he had been inside one of these rigs, and an uncanny feeling started settling over him. It was unlike anything he had ever experienced before. It closely resembled fear but was somehow different.

While waiting patiently for their breakfast, Rick kept asking if everyone had their radio turned on, afraid they might miss the call. Little by little everything started to overwhelm him. As the panic in him grew, he excused himself and went into the bathroom and became physically sick.

As they returned to the station where they continued waiting for the first call of the day, he asked over and over again, "Which truck is up for the next call?" Rick once again rushed to the bathroom to be sick again. Afterward he went outside for some fresh air and to have a cigarette, hoping it would help calm his nerves.

Suddenly, the overhead doors opened and the number 11 truck left for its first run. Rick stood there, waving, while deep inside he was thankful that it wasn't the truck he was assigned to.

Phyllis June came out to see if Rick was okay. He told her "I think I better go home. I'm not feeling very good." She told him that she understood and had thought that might be the case.

What Rick believed was going to be a great day of

reminiscing with old friends became almost a nightmare for him. The length of time it took for a call to come in was too much for him to handle. The truth of the matter was that too many emotions swirled around inside him while at the same time he was trying to deal with an extremely high level of anxiety. On his way home, Rick had to fight the blurred vision caused from the waves of his tears.

It was just one more, and final, awakening of how that part of Rick's past was gone forever and the realization that he had slipped further into this disease than he actually had thought.

You may be wondering why I put this chapter in the section of the book which talks about Memory People. It's because Rick is still "saving lives for a living." He's helping many survive the treachery of this disease by giving them the support they are in dire need of. And the truth of the matter is I know from firsthand experience that, by helping others, it brings a sense of self-healing for oneself. This fact helps him to face his own realistic future.

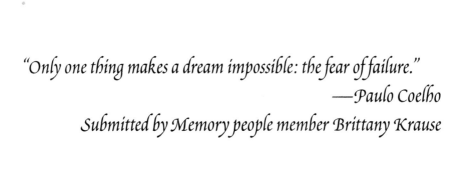

"Only one thing makes a dream impossible: the fear of failure."

—Paulo Coelho

Submitted by Memory people member Brittany Krause

Chapter 43

Video Journals

When his journey into the world of Alzheimer's began, Rick attempted to keep a daily journal of his experiences on his iPad. Unfortunately, due to the cognitive complications resulting from this disease, he found this exercise to be very difficult. He would miss a day or two, then maybe a week or even longer. At times it was just simply because he forgot. Other times he was remiss due to an inability to write out his thoughts. All of this culminated in his making the decision to make a video diary.

As expected there were a few difficulties at first, but ultimately he got on course. He soon realized this method was going to work for him.

He'd grab a cup of coffee, sit down in front of his computer, and start talking into the webcam, describing the ups and downs of his day. He would chat about the symptoms he was experiencing with Early-Onset Alzheimer's and what his biggest and smallest concerns were regarding everyone else facing the same dilemmas.

After a couple of weeks worth of recordings, he decided to ask his newfound Memory People family members if they would like him to share them.

Right off the bat they were extremely well received. He was told how helpful they were because they came from a patient's perspective.

It wasn't long before Rick was convinced that these videos were a win-win situation for everyone—caregivers, families, and those who are memory impaired themselves.

The next thing he knew he was being persuaded to market these videos to Assisted Living Facilities, Alzheimer's units, home care companies, nursing education programs, and anyone who might be caring for someone that is suffering from dementia.

The next step for Rick was to have a website created. With Leeanne's help, the site of www.whileistillcan.net was launched.

On this site is an introductory video, reviews, a short biography of Rick, and the details of how to download his video journal.

Once again Rick has found another valuable way to spread awareness of Alzheimer's to the general public.

"If I have learnt anything, it is that life forms no logical patterns. It is haphazard and full of beauties which I try to catch as they fly by for who knows whether any of them will ever return?"

—Margot Fonteyn

Submitted by Memory People member Phyllis June Phelps

Chapter 44

Phyllis June—Best Friend, Soul Mate, Caregiver, Loving Wife

It is becoming increasingly difficult in this day and age to find a couple who are as happily married as Rick and Phyllis June Phelps are. Since 1978 they have forged a close and loving relationship, sharing many of the same likes and dislikes, hobbies, and even the same manner of career. With the onset of Alzheimer's, however, Phyllis June has now found herself embracing a new role in their relationship, being a caregiver.

She has told me that the most difficult thing she has endured so far is not in the actual caring for Rick; it's in watching him go through the daily struggles and deterioration that this devastating disease has brought upon him. Sometimes she feels helpless as there's nothing she can do about it but offer comfort and "be there" for him.

For thirty-four years, Rick and Phyllis June have

always been a close couple. But now, she says, this disease has brought them to a point of being unconditionally united.

As guest speakers on a radio show called the *Caregiver Hour* hosted by Kim Linder out of Tampa Bay, Florida, Rick shared that Phyllis June knows him so well that when he finds himself at a loss for words, his wife finishes his sentences for him. That is something you can't teach a caregiver; this comes from years of true friendship.

Early-Onset Alzheimer's has brought their whole family closer in harmony. The Phelps family has always been tight-knit, but with Early-Onset Alzheimer's in the mix they find that they are now in closer harmony, gathering more frequently for family-oriented functions.

Without fail, they go out to dinner once or twice a month, take turns having cookouts or just visit one or the other's house to play cards or simply talk.

"It's almost as if we're all getting to know each other all over again," Phyllis June told me. In past years they always had busy schedules preventing this closeness, but now they seem to find a way to make time for each other.

As Rick's primary caregiver, Phyllis June has vowed to be by his side until, and if, she can no longer give him the proper medical attention he needs. Rick has already made his wishes very clear, that if that time comes, he wants to reside in an assisted living facility that will provide for his needs.

Phyllis June agonizes that Rick worries more about her than himself. She also knows that this is the type of man Rick has always been and one of the reasons she married him. He is a selfless human being, a rare commodity in anyone.

Becoming more acutely aware of her surroundings, Phyllis June has learned to cherish every single minute they spend together. She lives by a new motto, "Don't sweat the small stuff." They plan on making every day count to the fullest measure, no matter what it brings.

"Courage doesn't always roar. Sometimes courage is the quiet voice at the end of the day saying, 'I will try again tomorrow.'"

—Mary Anne Radmacher

Submitted by Memory People member Charlotte Bamsch

Chapter 45

Asking for Help

As a guest speaker at assisted living facilities and memory centers, etc., I've really enjoyed starting off by asking the listeners, "What do you think is one of the biggest mistakes a caregiver makes?"

The responses vary from shouting at a loved one to not taking care of the caregiver's own physical and mental health. The reality being that all of the above, and more, are correct.

In my opinion, the worst mistake a caregiver will make is not asking for help.

If asking for assistance becomes a priority, most of the other problems will likely be avoided. A caregiver needs to ascertain where they can find help right from the beginning of the diagnosis. Further down the road it will become obvious that, as the primary person in charge, they will barely have time to breathe.

Many caregivers not only don't have any family members who are willing to lend a hand, they also don't know where to go to locate help. One of the best places to go to find guidance in this undertaking is a local support group. The bond that develops between caregivers is something that is sincerely admirable. Within minutes a sense of brotherhood or sisterhood will start to wash over the group. Discussions will follow as the group shares what kind of assistance is needed and a variety of suggested resources will start flying around the room from all directions.

I also found that the area Chamber of Commerce has a plethora of information available. And of course the health section of the local newspaper will have listings of what is happening currently in your area.

Your family physician or a geriatric specialist, Veteran's Administration, or any local church for that matter may also provide some services or at least be able to point you in the right direction.

Become proactive. Train yourself to ask for help. There is no time like the present so, as I already stated, start early. A caregiver's campaign may seem like something that can be handled alone, but trust me: this becomes at least a two-person job as you travel further on down the road. It's not just you that you have to worry about. Your loved one's best interest is a major concern as well. So if you have to put part of your pride aside for you loved one's sake, so be it.

"Worrying does not take away tomorrow's troubles—it takes away today's peace."

—*Unknown Author*

Submitted by Memory People member Linda Casey–Overholt

Chapter 47

The Necessity of Patience

Patience is an essential ingredient in being a successful caregiver for people afflicted with Alzheimer's or any other form of dementia. In today's swift-paced world, it's difficult to discipline oneself to slow down. Before I became my father's primary caregiver I spent years working two jobs, averaging thirteen hours a day, plus another two hours behind the wheel going to and fro.

When I arrived in the world of caregiving I felt as if I was constantly driving through a school zone! It was quite the culture shock.

When caring for Alzheimer's patients, let yourself become part of their world, instead of trying to move them into yours.

I can't tell you how many mornings I spent trying to get my father ready for a doctor's appointment, finally asking myself, "Could he possibly move any slower?" On one occasion I decided he was trying to set a new Guinness Book of World Records for the slowest shave. I was forever calling the doctor's office to inform them that we were running late, as usual.

It takes a patient person to provide care when you're still able to move and process your thoughts quickly, but the person you're caring for cannot. It is understandably difficult to slow life down. I found myself constantly having to remind myself just how important it was not to rush my father, because all it ever accomplished was increasing his confusion prodigiously.

Being an impatient caregiver will only fill the room with anxiety and fear for all those involved. Keep your composure. It is not only important when these loved ones are moving in slow motion, but it also has much to do with keeping your cool while they're asking you the same question for the thirtieth time. Learning to bite your tongue and refrain from yelling, "I just told you that," all falls into the same category: forbearance. If you catch yourself speaking in an angry voice, take a step outside and breathe in some fresh air and kick a little dirt around. You must remain diligent in your awareness of knowing when you're about to lose your patience. When you feel that this is beginning to happen more and more often, it's only common sense to recognize this as a sign that you are in dire need of some respite care.

Patience is the state of endurance under extremely trying circumstances, and there's no better example of these circumstances than when caregiving.

I don't know who coined the phrase "Patience is a virtue," but I believe they might have been a caregiver at one point in their life.

"If you want others to be happy, practice compassion. If you want to be happy, practice compassion."

—Dalai Lama

Submitted by Memory People member Ruthie Rosenfeld

Chapter 48

Redirection

As you walk alongside your loved ones as they enter their last stages of Alzheimer's, redirecting their thoughts becomes almost impossible.

Previously, you may have been able to turn their fixations onto a different subject, but in the final stages of this terrible disease delusions and hallucinations become highly pronounced. You can no longer divert their train of thought for more than a few seconds at best.

When caring for Alzheimer's patients, you must learn to use redirection to your advantage. Knowing just when confusion is beginning to snowball straight into delusion and using simply phrased words, you can create a u-turn in their thought patterns. These are important skills for any caregiver to master.

When the afflicted patients begin speaking of a topic which makes absolutely no sense, casually interrupt with a quick question such as, "That color looks great on you; do you enjoy wearing that shirt?"

Steering the patient's mind onto a subject he or she can actually see, smell, or touch prevents hours of misery listening to meaningless chatter.

Anxiety could be playing a significant role in causing severe disorientation. If the patient has already been on a particular anxiety medication for a long period of time, it might be beneficial to discuss with his or her physician the possibility of increasing the dosage or trying something new. As symptoms of the disease advance you may soon find it necessary to realize the blessings of palliative care.

Among the many stories I have heard, one involved caregivers' mornings beginning with their patients believing, for instance, they were on a train. "Could you please tell me when the next stop is going to be? I believe that's where I have to get off." Attempting to reassure them that they were in their own home, their response was, "Come on! I can feel the train moving." If this should happen to you, it's best to just go along for the ride. The last thing anyone needs is to get patients' feathers all ruffled before the day even starts.

So, Dear Caregiver, hold on tight. From here on out, the ride will have fewer stops. Certain memories that drift through patients' minds just won't float away anymore. If a mental image has worked them into a frenzy, chances are it's going to last the entire day. It can even become difficult to convince them they have a home. They may constantly ask why they can't go to their parents' house or some other place that they believe is their abode.

All during the last stage of the disease, as you care for your loved one at home, you'll probably need a minimum of two people. Attempting to do everything yourself could erupt into a physical or mental fiasco, probably both. Create a schedule so that you know when relief is coming.

If these loved ones were able, they would surely advise you to take care of yourself so that when the inevitable comes to pass, and they die, you will hopefully be able to begin enjoying your own life again.

"The only man who never makes a mistake is the man who never does anything."

—Theodore Roosevelt

Submitted by Memory People member Anonymous

Chapter 49

Falling into Character

You will discover, as the disease of Alzheimer's progresses, that even the people closest to the ones afflicted with the disease will receive new identities. Names might change five times or more in a one-hour period.

You cannot prepare yourself ahead of time for the jarring moment when these loved ones look at you and have no recognition of who you are—it's nothing short of heartbreaking!

There will be moments of clarity though, and they will comprehend who you actually are, but these occasions will become few and far between. Watch closely as their facial expressions change and the profound sorrow they feel will be revealed.

Remember; it's not their fault. Accept the role they have you in and assume your new identity. First, you may become a close relative—maybe a brother, sister, uncle, aunt, or other family member deep from their past. Later you will assume still another role. Names seem to be randomly drawn out of a hat.

Most often my father believed I was his dad. I learned to work this to my advantage. Listening to me with deeper respect, he would ask, "Dad, do I have to take all these pills?" and then I would gently but firmly respond,

"Yes, son, please take them all and don't make me get your mother involved." Playing the role can help both parties. I had become "Dad" 80 percent of the time. There's15 percent spent as a brother, and then being recognized as his son dwindled to a diminutive final 5 percent.

As the oldest of seventeen children, my dad would most often ask for his brother Alfie, who was the second oldest. Well, the reality is, Alfie had passed away shortly after WWII. If I even attempted to tell him this, he would become extremely upset, yelling, "How could you people not even tell me about my brother's funeral? I can't believe I missed it." Instead I would tell him, "Alfie just left. He said something about being back in the morning."

Go with the flow. Playing along with the current scenario will be instrumental in comforting and relieving some of the stress. You must learn to quickly adapt; they did.

"The best advantage to telling the truth is that you never have to remember what you said."

—Mark Twain

Submitted by Memory People member Anastasia Ryan

Chapter 50

The Therapeutic Lie

Never argue with someone who is memory impaired. First and foremost you will never win the argument! Secondly, you're only going to end up tormenting the both of you. Just go with the flow. Even if they're making absolutely no sense at all, just agree with them.

If suddenly one day you find that you are now called "Bob," then just become Bob! Telling them they're mistaken will only send them deeper into their own confusion, creating a heavy bout of anxiety and nervousness. As the caregiver, this is exactly what you are trying to avoid.

I experienced many evenings when my dad would say to me, "It's starting to get dark outside. If I don't get home soon, my mother is going to start worrying about me." Now, instead of telling him that he was now a man in his eighties and that his mother had passed away some twenty years ago, I would calmly tell him, "I just talked to your mother on the telephone a little while ago. She knows you're spending the night here with me. Everything is going to be okay." More often than not, by the next morning, he wouldn't even remember having been worried in the first place.

A year or so ago I was confronted by a fellow caregiver who was very upset with me. She couldn't believe that I was actually telling her to go home and straight-out lie to her husband. I tried to explain to her that she needed to do what's best for herself and her husband, but she didn't want any part of this. Six weeks later, however, I received a phone call from this same lady letting me know she had been at the end of her rope and decided to take my advice. With a smile in her voice she admitted that it worked; things had now become a lot easier for her.

I used to describe this as telling "little white lies." But recently I met someone who told me that I should call them "therapeutic lies." I couldn't have agreed more.

Keeping a loved one's anxiety under control is vital for someone who has Alzheimer's or any other kind of dementia-related disease. So if you have to bend the truth a little by telling a therapeutic fib, so be it. Consider it to be an act of love.

"Tongue biting can be difficult, but sometimes it is for the best."
—Unknown Author
Submitted by Memory People member Robert Euton

Chapter 51

Communication

Once afflicted with Alzheimer's, patients will start losing their communication skills. Unfortunately, it's inevitable. As a caregiver you need to adjust your speaking techniques throughout the different stages of the disease, adapting to changes as they occur.

Learn to face the patients directly, talking to them as if they're reading your lips. I'll be the first to admit I was guilty of saying something to my dad as I was walking into another room, only to have to return and speak in a more direct manner, making sure he clearly understood me.

Be patient with them and yourself. This matter gets very frustrating and tiresome. Learn to stay away from subjects that might upset them. I won't make a list of subjects to avoid as this is unique to each individual. You'll know which ones they are. If you don't, you'll quickly figure them out by the other responses you get as time goes by.

In some of the more orthodox crime detective practices

of solving mysteries, trained investigators are taught to always concentrate on asking the five Ws: who, what, when, where, and why. As a caregiver you will soon discover that your daily routine involves the perpetual task of solving many mysteries. But on the other hand, these are also five words you will want to refrain from using at certain times. Common sense should be telling you when to back away from any questions which are incorporated with the five Ws:

- Who are you upset with?
- What would you like to eat?
- When are you going to wash up?
- Where do you think you're going?
- Why are you crying?

There are many other letters in the alphabet besides Ws to worry about. The point being, when you see that they are already having difficulties don't begin making inquiries that you know they probably won't be able to answer, likely causing further turmoil. Just use the five Ws as a rule of thumb to hold in abeyance in the back of your mind.

The short-term memory will gradually dissipate from the mind of your Alzheimer's patients. Whatever happened just a few minutes ago never occurred in the mind of these victims. However, the long-term memory survives until the later stage of the disease.

My father's memories of his many siblings and buddies from the past always seemed to remain fresh. This has me believing that if old friends are still available, any social interaction with them, even if it's just a weekly phone conversation, could be very therapeutic, possibly helping to keep patients' long-term memory and communication skills viable longer.

Caregivers should make it their goal to maintain patients' verbal abilities, extending them as far into the disease as feasible. Once the patient stops speaking, everything else begins accelerating downhill from that point.

Do what you can to encourage quiet social visits or phone conversations with figures from the past. Patients may hang up the receiver, instantly forgetting whom they just talked with, but the mental exercise of that conversation just might keep their long-term gears turning. (You'll want to stay in earshot range of the confabulation just in case they begin to become flustered.)

A fellow caregiver explained to me that her mother is constantly asking if she can move back to her hometown. Her mom believes that everything would go back to the way things were forty-some years ago and she would be living the same lifestyle of her younger days. Now we all know this isn't possible, but what would be the harm in letting her exchange fifteen minutes of friendly chitchat, reminiscing with an old sidekick from the days she can still remember?

At one point during my dad's illness, I began noticing randomly dialed numbers showing up on my phone bill. It's probably a good idea to dial the phone number for them yourself so you don't end up paying fifty dollars worth of international calls!

Researchers have discovered that telling them stories often sparks their imagination. These stories can be used as a catalyst for releasing thoughts that are trapped deep in the back of their minds, collecting dust. You might ask,

"Where does someone get such stories?" Well, remember the old saying about listening to your elders? Well, this is a perfect place to begin. If you're caring for your parents, the stories that were told to you throughout the years are ideal to recite back to them. These tales have special meanings to your loved ones. Even if you happen to tell a story wrong and get corrected, you have successfully induced a conversation. By knocking off the cobwebs from those pathways traveling through their brain, you may assist their mind in them telling you a story you never heard before.

Sadly, people suffering from dementia arrive at a point where they can no longer recall many of the facts about their own life, but they seem quite adept at constructing a new reality.

It takes a lot of energy, learning, and patience to reckon with Alzheimer's patients, but you can certainly enrich their lives by sharing the give and take, one story at a time.

While caring for your loved ones, learn to cherish the conversations you're now having, because when they are gone, trust me, they will truly be missed.

When they say things you know are wrong, learn not to correct them. This only puts them in a state of confusion. Also, keep your statements short and simple, but please don't demean them by talking to them as if they are children.

If you're giving them instructions, only direct them to do one thing at a time. If you say to them, "You need to wash your hands and brush your teeth so we can go to the doctor," that will be too much for them to absorb.

Mention one step at a time. You might even get out of the house sooner.

Eventually you'll start noticing they won't stay on the same subject very long. They will stop in the middle of a sentence, then forget what they were saying. Pay close attention to their "body language." You'll soon learn their facial expressions: pain, depression, confusion, and love. They're all in there. Be patient and loving. It is as frustrating for them as it is for you, maybe more so.

"Worry does not empty tomorrow of its troubles. It empties today of its strength."

—Leo Buscaglia

Submitted by Memory People member Kathy Turner Montgomery

Chapter 52

Pain of Depression

Isolation and despair are two of the first words that come to mind when considering the many emotions involved in dealing with Alzheimer's. The hopelessness of caring for victims of Alzheimer's, knowing they are on a one-way street heading toward their concluding address, brings about a constantly cloudy forecast.

It's not easily understood how someone could feel alone while caring for a patient 24/7. But when treasured conversations dissolve, and you as the caregiver are barely recognized, trust me, loneliness creeps in and surrounds you like a dense sea fog. Riding high on this fog is the feeling of isolation from the rest of the normal world.

As a caregiver, it is not easy to come by adequate sleep. Unfortunately, depression is always strongest when the caregiver is overcome with fatigue. These are a few signs to watch for:

- Constant sadness

- Hopelessness
- Disruptive sleep patterns
- Fatigue
- Feeling worthless or guilty
- Significant weight change
- Loss of concentration
- Apathy

It's easy to turn to alcohol and medications for escape, but don't succumb to this temptation. This only adds weight to the burden of fatigue. Physical and mental exhaustion from substance abuse prevents the caregiver from ever catching up.

Sharing your feelings with a support group might do wonders. There are also several online chat rooms in which caregivers have an opportunity to vent. Keep in mind though, talking about stressors doesn't necessarily mend them. It's often necessary to go back to the origin of the problem.

If you're worried, remember, it's only natural. Try not to let it beat you up. Stay in touch with family and friends. Sometimes after a simple phone conversation, you'll feel a burden lift from your chest, at least long enough to catch your second breath. If necessary, talk with your physician. There's nothing to be ashamed of; you're doing a job most people wouldn't even attempt in the first place.

Understandably, depression is also widespread among those afflicted with Alzheimer's disease. In most cases, their downheartedness grows as their memory loss and the inability to live a normal life increases.

I've talked with many fellow caregivers who have told me that their loved ones go through a period of uncontrollable weeping, sometimes to the point that they are left almost breathless.

Throughout the years of caring for my dad, I often found him sitting at our kitchen table with tears in his eyes. This would happen most often during the early afternoon, a time of day when he really should have been at his best. During his brief moments of clarity he became acutely aware of what was happening to him, and waves of sadness would sweep over him.

I witnessed how hard he struggled with his pride, trying desperately to hold himself together, especially in my presence. But it seemed that when my sister was with him, he would often drop his guard and occasionally cry for over an hour.

Persistent crying is, without doubt, a sign of depression and is an issue that should be brought immediately to the attending physician's attention.

Also, don't forget to attempt to divert their thoughts onto more pleasant memories from the past. Reminisce about something that has some kind of happy emotional attachment to them. This will be a much better strategy than to perpetually ask them, "What's wrong?" But unfortunately, with this disease, there comes a time when redirection will no longer do its job.

Try to decipher whether or not the tears are flowing from emotional or physical pain. Hopefully, this is something the physician will thoroughly investigate prior to treatment for major depression. Remember that it is well known that while someone is depressed they may also endure severe headaches along with other frequent body pains.

Antidepressant medications have been very effective in

treating people suffering from Alzheimer's. As I've stated before, I truly believe that if their anxiety and depression are under control, they will manage a hundred times better throughout the course of the disease.

Do your best to maintain a realistic expectation of what your loved one can or cannot do. Expecting too much will only bring on additional frustration, possibly causing both of you to become more emotionally upset.

Please make sure you are not blaming yourself. Take comfort in knowing that these symptoms are generated from the disease itself. As the caregiver, actively anticipate these breakdowns taking place along the road of your journey.

It's always devastating to watch someone you care about cry incessantly, but keep in mind that hugs were invented to let someone know you love them without even saying a word.

"Laughter and tears are both responses to Frustration and Exhaustion. I myself prefer to laugh since there is less cleaning up to do afterward."

~ Kurt Vonnegut
Submitted by Memory People member Jackie Leight Cerqua

Chapter 53

Caregiver Stress

Inside of a leaflet dealing with caregiver stress I discovered a Cosmopolitan magazine-type questionnaire. I answered seven out of eight questions "yes" only to read at the bottom, "If you answered any of the above questions yes, you are probably experiencing Caregiver Stress." I could feel my blood pressure begin to rise as I read that presumptive evaluation.

I've always emphasized that all Alzheimer's patients react differently, and I'm convinced this is also true for caregivers. A large amount of tension comes from the caregivers themselves feeling guilty, thinking that they are not performing an adequate or acceptable job. I offer here a truism: "There's no such thing as a perfect caregiver."

This is easier said than done but take a moment to analyze your situation. Identify what you can reasonably expect to change or not change. Then concentrate on what is fixable and try not to let the rest overcome you.

Another risk for a caregiver is the threat of becoming physically exhausted. Keep a sharp eye out for signs of:

- Irritability
- Loneliness
- Feeling overwhelmed
- Chronic headaches or body pains
- Weakness
- Dizziness
- Nausea or vomiting
- Weight change up or down
- Heavy perspiration

When such physical symptoms occur, it's more than likely time to ask for help and train yourself to accept it.

Being a caregiver is a lonely and arduous job. Therefore, it is especially important that you maintain your own personal health. One problem will most likely be that almost every spare second of your day is already consumed, so you begin to cancel your medical appointments. Also, the financial burden of caring for an Alzheimer's patient may result in no longer refilling your own much-needed prescriptions.

Please try to remember that through all these difficulties, caring for your loved one does have its rewards. The fact that you're needed makes you feel worthy and helps you learn to appreciate life more fully. Ernest Hemingway advised, "To endure, one must laugh." You must keep your sense of humor and chuckle at the unbelievable things that are bound to happen.

Keep in mind, company employees covered by the "Federal Family and Medical Leave Act" may be able to take up to twelve weeks of "unpaid" leave per year to care for ailing relatives.

Make a habit of setting a certain amount of time aside for yourself each week. Pamper yourself, even if it's only for a couple of hours.

"Some of the best conversations I had with my father were in silence, when only his heart was able to speak."

Written by Memory People member Beth McCormack

Chapter 54

Stubbornness

A good example of stubbornness resulting from Alzheimer's Disease can be seen during preparations for a visit to the doctor's office. My dad may have had an appointment at 2:00 p.m., but I would inform him it was at 1:00 p.m. Just maybe we would arrive on time.

Between his nervousness and his anxiety (and mine) it was difficult to motivate the man. He would insist he had to go to the bathroom twenty times before leaving. We were lucky to make it there at all.

You have to realize that when Alzheimer's patients refuse to do something for you, it's probably because it is less embarrassing for them to abstain than to attempt the act, risking failing a simple task. Being uncooperative is easier for them than looking foolish. Keep in mind that their attitude may very well be induced by the brain impairment caused by the disease.

Now, if patients are stubborn prior to the development of Alzheimer's, the caregivers hands will likely be extra full. Most lifelong characteristics remain with them throughout the course of the disease.

Common excuses:

- I already did that
- I'll do it later
- I don't want to
- I don't have time

Don't take these remarks personally. Nobody likes to look foolish. If patients are being stubborn try asking them again to do whatever task is at hand when you're positive only the two of you are present. Things might flow a little smoother. There will be times when it doesn't matter what you say or do. Never force an issue to the point of argument, just let the dust die down and try again later.

"I've gone to look for myself, If you should see me before I get back, please keep me here!"

—Unknown Author

Submitted by Memory People member Tess LeBlanc

Chapter 55

Wandering

During the course of caring for my father with Alzheimer's, I was awakened at 2:30 a.m. to the familiar clanking of my father's walker. I didn't move a muscle as I listened closely, assuring myself that what I had heard was Dad moving around. Suddenly, the distinctive sound of the back door opening brought me instantly to my feet. Approaching him quickly but gently so as not to startle him I asked, "Where are we going?" as if we were a team. "I've got to take a leak," was his retort.

Dad's confusion had him believing he was still in his childhood home. There the only plumbing had been in the outhouse in the backyard.

As you can imagine, this was an extremely dangerous situation. Just the darkness alone would have magnified his confusion to the point where he might not have found his way back to the house. He might have fallen, lying there for hours. Morning would dawn and he would have been nowhere to be found.

My father wasn't very mobile and in many ways that was fortunate. He needed that noisy, rattling walking device which, thankfully, was louder than a provoked rattlesnake. Believe me, I went through my share of warning devices that alerted me when he was on the move.

First I tried a baby monitor, hiding it in his bedroom closet. I was quite impressed with its clarity. It picked up every little sound; it even resounded with the toilet flushing. The downside, however, was that I had to lie there night after night listening to him snore. As you can imagine I quickly moved on to another apparatus. This one proved to be less than a stroke of genius: stuffed parrots with motion detectors built inside. They were beyond obnoxious as they squawked loud enough to wake the dead! Positioned at the front and back door, they worked extremely well except for the fact that they almost gave anyone passing by a heart attack. (Including me!)

I finally moved on to placing deadbolts on the tops of doorframes. The only problem I had with this was that Dad occasionally locked me out of the house.

Find out what works best for your situation. There are many variables when dealing with memory-impaired patients. Remember, every Alzheimer's patient responds differently. As the disease advances, communication skills quickly evaporate. Be creative. Try placing signs throughout the house indicating which way to turn to go to which room. I positioned a sign on the bathroom door with great success. (You can write it out or just place a picture of a toilet on it.)

Many times when you find them roaming about it's only because they couldn't remember what they originally started out to do. Random background noise could also be a contributing factor. For instance the sound of someone knocking on a television program might send them to the front door. One more step and they're outside wandering away.

Many Alzheimer's organizations have a "safe return program" which provides patients with ID bracelets. Also, if they're still carrying a wallet, make sure that it contains a list of contact numbers and addresses.

Use today's modern technology to your advantage. When it comes to preventing and/or handling patients who are at risk for wandering, check out the many websites designed for caregivers and family members alike. File vital information that would be needed in case a loved one wanders from home. This file should contain current photos, addresses, phone numbers, and all crucial background information needed for police departments and possibly search and rescue teams. This data can be downloaded in a minute's time.

Update their data approximately every six months. There's no doubt that many Alzheimer's patients get shuffled around. For instance, I know of a family in which the daughter tried taking care of an afflicted parent but only to find out, months later, she just couldn't handle it. Soon the patient ended up at another offspring's home, and then an adult facility. You can almost count on most of the paperwork and vital information being lost during a shuffle like that.

Due to my father's severe weight loss during his last year I found myself updating his photo ID pretty frequently. Many of his past acquaintances would never have recognized him.

Obviously, we need to use all of the new technology available to us, such as locator bands which produce a miniaturized single-purpose cell phone designed to be worn like a wristwatch. Not to be mistaken for Dick Tracy's two-way radio watch, this device, only upon activation, dials 911 and reports its location. It works solely upon existing emergency 911 systems and needs to be charged approximately two hours every week.

As I said, my dad wasn't very mobile, but in opposite cases, accidents can happen in microseconds. One foot over the threshold and there is no telling what could happen next. Being lost will compound their confusion, and they might become belligerent or verbally abusive. Strangers just trying to help them might be in for a handful.

Temperature extremes and inclement weather should be a major concern for any caregiver who is watching over an elderly person. The body's ability to produce its own heat declines with age. In addition, those suffering from Alzheimer's or other forms of dementia bring on additional worries during a cold spell.

You'd think that you wouldn't have to worry about loved ones venturing outside into freezing temperatures. After all, who would want to go face the elements and be anesthetized by the blistering cold? But the fact remains that any change in climate will cause an interruption in their daily routine bringing on heavier bouts of confusion. Suddenly you may find them moving from room to room searching for additional warmth. Be aware that hypothermia is a danger lurking around many corners.

Hypothermia comes from the lowering of the body temperature to ninety-five degrees Fahrenheit (F) or below. I know that my father's body temperature would normally stay around ninety-seven degrees (F), which put him almost halfway to being at risk.

Even in moderately cool temperatures around forty-five degrees (F) hypothermia can occur. All it takes is the human body becoming chilled from being caught in the rain or even soaked from their own sweat. Make no mistake; this is a medical emergency that requires immediate attention. Some indications will be: decreased heart and respiratory rates, slow reflexes, shivering, and additional confusion. It may also cause the victim to refrain from seeking shelter as they suffer from oxygen deprivation causing an inability for them to comprehend that they are in dire need of help. They may likewise lose the ability to communicate how they actually feel.

If you're not living with persons you're caring for 24/7, explain to their neighbors what the situation is and ask them to check on them and call you immediately if they see them wandering away from home.

Even if they live in a care facility, the concern about them wandering doesn't go away. The official medical term for this is "elopement." Always look into each living establishment's ability to cope with this before deciding to place your loved one there. Keep in mind that even if he or she never had a history of wandering, this doesn't mean it's not going to happen in the near future. An interesting diversion can be to hide a favorite "going out hat" or purse, suppressing the desire to leave.

Do your best to make sure patients reside in comfortable surroundings. You don't want them to become cold in the middle of the night, causing them to roam around, possibly getting into trouble.

The dangers involved when a wandering memory-impaired patient is unsupervised are endless.

"*Life is uncertain, eat dessert first.*"

—*Ernestine Ulmer*

Submitted by Memory People member Michelle Hudson Yoxall

Chapter 56

Appetite

"I just ate an hour ago." This is a declaration you, as a caregiver to Alzheimer's patients, will likely hear two or three times a week.

Malnutrition is a major concern in regards to people afflicted with Alzheimer's Disease. This should be utmost in your mind. Keeping mealtime in a routine is a rule that should be made early on and remain throughout the course of the disease. Breakfast, lunch, and dinner kept on a set schedule helps keep things simple, therefore more bearable for a deteriorating mind.

A wise caregiver friend of mine is regimented in having dinner on the table every night at 6:30 p.m. sharp! This way, when his father inevitably goes into his address about how he had already eaten, he asks him to take a gander at his watch, reminding him what time they always have supper. 'Nuf said.

Actually sitting and eating together makes mealtimes go much smoother. Keep it simple. Do not give multiple choices for dinner; otherwise you will have to reschedule dinner for later. Again, simplicity is the rule.

The more confused Alzheimer's patients are, before eating, the more often you will find large quantities of food left on their plates. If they protest that there's too much in front of them at the outset, you might try more modest portions or even a smaller-sized plate.

Stick with whatever routine to which they're accustomed. Whether it's a television broadcasting the news in the background or a quiet mellow atmosphere, whatever works, stick with it. Otherwise, revert back to the old trial and error, and eventually you'll find the right combination.

I'm once again advising you to pay close attention and learn as much as possible from these patients. Remember, their reactions will be your best teacher. In the long run it should noticeably ease stress for everyone involved.

If weight loss should occur, it's important to apprise their physician immediately. Depression could very well be one of many contributing factors.

Don't assume the worst, but you should know this could be the advancement of the disease itself. Once again, pay close attention, especially to their swallowing and speech.

Getting pills down will eventually become a problem. If so, try using a thicker beverage to help push the medications down, something like tomato juice or even applesauce or ice cream. When swallowing pills, try having them keep the chin down against their chest, not facing up. Actually looking up while swallowing will open the windpipe, but closes the esophagus, which is the complete opposite of what you want to do. This also helps to stifle a gag reflex. "Ensure" or some other brand of high-calorie supplement might also prove useful in helping to keep a pound or two of weight on, supplying valuable nutrients.

Another ground rule: make sure your patient does not get constipated! Poison, due to blockage caused by constipation, can be very serious. Don't depend upon their perceptions. According to them they were fine "two days ago."

Don't rely on what an Alzheimer's victim is telling you. Somehow, constantly drill that into your head. You have to take matters into your own hands and make a judgment call, though heaven knows you have enough on your plate already.

"Don't be afraid to give your best to what seemingly are small jobs. Every time you conquer one, it makes you that much stronger."

——Dale Carnegie

Submitted by Holly Beth Michaels
who helped immensely with the writing of this book.

Chapter 57

Incontinence

Incontinence is an inevitable part of Alzheimer's. Each situation will be unique, so there is no way to predict when, during the disease process, this will occur. Naturally, most people become squeamish at the thought of handling this, but remember—this is not Bio-Hazardous material.

Like everything else a caregiver undertakes, caring for people who are incontinent is a learning process.

It is a known fact that Alzheimer's patients will arrive at a point where they lose control of their bladder or bowels, most likely both. When this happens caregivers are advised to institutionalize their loved ones. Even so, countless families continue caring for them at home until their final days.

Incontinence begins with some occasional accidents, possibly because they couldn't make it to the bathroom quickly enough or were unable to remove their clothing in time. I dressed my father with pants that had an elastic waistband: pull up, pull down, quick and easy.

Help your patients preserve as much dignity as possible. Train yourself to say things like, "Oops, you spilled something on your pants," rather than, "Oh my! I see you had another accident."

Think of Ronald Reagan and Christopher Reeves. One was a U.S. President and the other Superman. These were the very essence of people of dignity. However, the need for adult diapers became necessary. In no way did this detract from their honor and respectability.

Incontinence pads, adult diapers, and other such health care products are intended to keep the patients' bottoms clean and protected along with furniture, clothing, and other consequential yet replaceable objects. Keep in mind, you're crossing the personal barrier of self-respect. However, as the caregiver, it has to be your decision when to start using these products. Incontinence care is more difficult with Alzheimer's patients because of their inability to make right choices. They may for instance suddenly rip their nappies off, not understanding why they are suddenly wearing such an item.

In the event you may wish to include them on an outing, keep a bag packed at all times containing clothing, wipes, and any of the incontinence products you may find necessary.

The dreaded fear of the cleanup is far worse than the actual task. Once you get past that squeamish point, the routine becomes easier. Keep things organized; put everything in one convenient place so you will not need to dash out of the room in the middle of a cleanup, only to return finding a mess everywhere.

You should keep a daily record of the time of day

patients have bowel movements or urinate. This way you'll learn when they should be seated on the toilet.

Also, be sure to pay close attention to their skin as a little redness can quickly develop into a nasty bedsore.

Lastly, make sure you have latex gloves that fit. By the time you finally get those darn things on you could be dealing with pure chaos everywhere.

"There is in every true person's heart a spark of heavenly fire, which kindles up, beams and blazes, in the dark hour of adversity."

—Washington Irving

Submitted by Memory People member Tia Bookless.

Chapter 58

Problems with Bathing

Feelings of pride, dignity, and embarrassment loom large in the matter of bathing Alzheimer's patients. Whether it's self-consciousness or loss of independence, this task must be handled with the utmost compassion.

If you're familiar with their already-established daily routines, try to continue following that pattern for the sake of the patients involved.

My father was one who first ate breakfast and then shaved and showered. I learned how much more difficult it was to bathe him in the evenings, always telling me how he had already washed that morning.

As I have said, it's best to keep all Alzheimer's patients in a daily routine. More likely than not, you'll run into the situation where they might have an early morning doctor's appointment. If you plan on bathing them that morning, chances of your arriving on time are extremely slim.

There are times when bathing in the evening might work to your advantage. Here are some suggestions on how to preserve Alzheimer's patients' privacy: try placing a large towel or robe over their shoulders and one over their lap, then try washing under the towel. It's important to have bathing items ready and laid out, within easy reach so you won't have to stop and leave the patients unattended during the middle of the procedure. Never leave them alone. It only takes a microsecond for something bad to happen. Install whatever safety devices are needed: handrails, traction strips, shower bench, and a handheld shower sprayer—these are a must for proper rinsing. I'm sure you know how to prepare the basics: water temperature, towels, and shampoo. Try sticking to the same brands. They will get accustomed to certain aromas.

There are ways to softly coax them into bathing. Tell them you would like to wash their back, "Please remove your shirt." Once their shirt is off say, "I'd like to wash your feet. Is it okay if I take your shoes off?" Keep up this approach until you finally have them in their birthday suit.

There will be good days and bad days. If you're upsetting them too much, you might want to bring into play the old-fashioned sponge bath. You don't want to overstress the issue. If the experience becomes too traumatic, it might be even more difficult the next time.

Please, do not tell them they stink. This is an approach they'll only find offensive and will get you absolutely nowhere. Nobody likes to be insulted, even if it's true.

Bathing them two or three times a week should be sufficient unless they become incontinent. Then you'll have to wash and observe their skin condition daily. Make sure pressure sores don't arise and become infected. If you notice any area you're worried about, contact their physician right away.

Try to make their bathing experience as pleasurable as possible. It's best to have the same person do all the bathing rather than different faces. Keep to the same routine as much as possible. There will be times when they flat out refuse. As the caregiver, you must be flexible; an hour or two later might bring totally different results.

"Please don't be afraid of me. I'm still me, just a slightly less fabulous version of me. Keep that in mind and we'll both be fine."
Written by Memory People member Karen Bell Eisenberg

Chapter 59

Shadowing

Shadowing is the act of an Alzheimer's or dementia victim attempting to keep his or her caregiver in sight at all times.

During the years of caring for my dad, I could often feel his warm breath on the back of my neck. I didn't even have to turn around! He followed me around like a small child clinging to its mother's apron strings.

During the rare occasions that I would leave him with a volunteer respite caregiver he would constantly ask where I was, sometimes more than twenty times in an hour! Obviously this was quite unnerving to the volunteer. This behavior began right around the same time he started showing signs of Sundowner's (Sundown Syndrome).

There is a lot of fear involved for someone who is suffering from being memory impaired. People living with Alzheimer's can experience this all day long. They finally reach the stage where they just don't feel safe alone anymore. I've always said, "Controlling their anxiety is half the battle."

The primary caregiver is like a security blanket, a lifeline, the center of their universe; and they want to always be with them, following them everywhere, and I do mean everywhere! Bathrooms included. At times the patient will mimic the caregiver, making for an unsettling experience.

If this should happen to you, attempt to make a note of the time of day it occurs. Find a repetitious activity to keep them entertained, such as folding laundry, a jigsaw puzzle, or even playing Solitaire.

If the person is still able to chew and swallow, you might want to try something referred to as "Gum Therapy." It's worth a try. A single stick of chewing gum might land you a peaceful thirty minutes.

Many a night's rest was interrupted for me when I would awaken to discover my dad standing there staring at me. He would actually awaken me just to ask if I was sleeping!

Shadowing is just one of the myriads of symptoms Alzheimer's victims go through, but for the caregiver it can definitely be one of the more unnerving ones.

"Let prayer be in your Heart and singing in your Soul and laughter be your best medicine."

—*Unknown Author*
Submitted by Memory People member Pauline Baker

Chapter 60

Hallucinations and Delusions

"They're breaking into the building next door! All the tools behind the building are being stolen!" These are the types of very common hallucinations which manifest themselves in the minds of Alzheimer's victims.

This is only one of the cruel effects of Alzheimer's and can be very hard for the caregiver to bear. Even after as much as a decade of caregiving, this can continue to be one of its most heartrending facets.

If you are a caregiver, you will likely find that hallucinations and delusions are two of the most strenuous memory disorders to contend with. You'll really need to tap into your reserve of endurance in order to avoid losing patience. Exhibiting signs of frustration will make matters worse.

On a past Memorial Day weekend, my father took a gander out the kitchen window and asked, "What are those twenty-five people doing having dinner in our backyard?" Well, I would never have even considered inviting that many guests. I wisely kept my dad in a simple routine lifestyle, keeping all confusion to a minimum. This is the most important undertaking when assisting a patient with Alzheimer's: Keep it simple.

If this happens to you, remember that your patient truly believes he or she is witnessing something. Don't turn it into a debate. Period! Instead, be affirming with, "I just went out and checked. They must have just left." You might have to take a walk outside and circle the house. At this point you probably need some fresh air and some good ol' dirt kicking anyway. Whatever you do, don't get into an argument. It will only twist things further, and you both will likely be headed for hours of extended madness.

You will find that this is one of the most difficult situations to deal with as caregiver. There were many times it became necessary for me to call my sister for backup. You'll find there are times you cannot handle these delusions one more minute. Like a "horse rode too hard and put up wet," you may need open pasture, and a friend or relative can come to the rescue. The point? Without meaning to, Alzheimer's patients can use you up. You may consider going for a long drive but, with someone trustworthy at the helm, you may just decide to sleep, simply too mentally and physically exhausted to go anywhere.

It's amazing how the "untrue" will remain in patients' minds, sometimes for days! Then the next moment, something that just happened two minutes ago no longer exists. What they believe they're seeing, smelling, or even tasting is as real to them as the love you have for them. This love will keep you going.

"Oh, Great Manitou of all families . . . send our love to our children's children. Let them listen closely . . . it will be our voices they hear in their hearts. They will become strong too, as we are strong now in our sorrow. Our memories will dance and leap triumphantly as others remember our lives and the many paths that we walked on this earth together. I have never believed otherwise. Let them all step back in time and experience our strength."

Written by Memory People member Kathleen Dean

Chapter 61

Informing loved ones that they have Alzheimer's

Should we tell our loved ones that they are suffering from Alzheimer's? This is a dilemma all caregivers must face sooner or later.

First, let's consider what stage of the disease the patients are currently in. Obviously, the earlier the stage, the more they will be able to comprehend. But as the disease progresses, constantly informing them that they are showing symptoms may have little or no advantage. Each caregiver has to use his or her own judgment pertaining to what they feel is best in their own circumstance. There is no "how to" manual of rights and wrongs when it comes to dealing with this disease. Each patient responds differently.

At first, it's important for patients to have the opportunity to decide their own future care and the care of their dependents. Also, this may sound funny, but they will actually need some time to grieve about being given this dreadful diagnosis. This is a valid stage for them to walk through which may help them to determine what choices are to be made in their own behalf.

You will always want to do what's best for them. Your initial reaction is naturally going to be to protect them from any further pain or distress. If you feel it's best not to awaken the memories of the diagnosis, make sure to tell other family members and friends so that you are all on the same page.

Now if you desire to go the other route, reminding them of the reason they are constantly confused, make sure it is done in a sensitive manner and then reassure them that you will always be there for them. When discussing the matter, see how it goes at first. If you see that they are becoming upset, back off. Usually the best time of day for them is going to be between 10:00 a.m. and 3:00 p.m. Remember, this disease not only affects their ability to comprehend, it also affects their power to communicate. It's only fair that they should be given the opportunity to express concerns about what is happening to them.

I've always stated that denial is a symptom of the disease which seems to affect everyone involved. It's possible they might never actually accept there is something wrong with them. This is one situation where telling them may send them into a whirlwind of anxiety, doing more harm than good. If you are the person who initially discovers strange behaviors or their acting out of character, then I would advise you to call their doctor, thus giving the physician a heads up that you feel there's something potentially wrong. But it is very common for patients to instruct their doctors not to tell anyone about their diagnosis. This is one of the problems with the disease which may become a little bit taboo for the physician. You may have a better chance of being brought in on the diagnosis if you're the one who initially raised the concern.

If you are certain that your loved one should always be informed what is happening to them, be prepared to repeat yourself for many years to come. In the case of my father I elected not to keep telling him. I felt there was no reason to bring up a subject matter that was followed by a wave of depression. Even if it lasted only ten minutes, that's still ten minutes long.

"Walking with a Friend in the dark is better than walking alone in the light."

—Helen Keller

Submitted by Memory People member Patrick Rush

Chapter 62

Doctor Visits

While being my father's caregiver as he suffered from Alzheimer's Disease, there were many hard lessons I had to learn. One example that stands out in my mind is the hardship of keeping doctor's appointments. I truly don't believe we ever had even one such date go smoothly.

Once trying to kill two birds with one stone, I tried scheduling an appointment for myself at the same time since both our doctors were in the same building. Big mistake. I had Dad checked in to see his physician first, afterward I asked the nurse or receptionist to please keep an eye on him while I walked down the hall to my examination room. When I returned, Dad was nowhere to be found! If my blood pressure wasn't high before, it was certainly off the charts now! Dashing out the main door I found him roaming the parking lot, a very dangerous place for anyone with dementia. The anxiety that results from a foray like this can actually last for days.

My advice here is this: If at all possible, have a third

party accompany you to appointments of any kind. This way, if you need to speak with the doctor in private or even use the bathroom alone, the extra person can attend to your loved one.

Another deep concern that I have regards a very common complaint I hear from Alzheimer's caregivers: "I'm not receiving enough help from our doctor." I certainly understand their vexation. I found myself switching doctors myself. It's my opinion that since there is no cure, some physicians become stagnant and blase. They are simply not aggressive enough. They don't seem to realize that there are *two* people in need of care: the patient and the caregiver.

Please know it's extremely difficult switching to a new doctor. There's a feeling of security in staying with the same one for a lengthy period of time. Then there is also a concern about hurting the doctor's feelings after building a doctor-patient relationship. You will need to get over this.

If it should become necessary to find a new doctor be sure that expectations can be reasonably met. Caregivers become overtired and worn down, so only make this decision with careful thought when well rested.

Be aware that changing physicians will be time consuming and may incur additional costs such as copying and transferring medical files along with requiring new lab tests.

Your first question should be, "What type of doctor treats Alzheimer's patients?" A primary care physician should be able to handle most of your needs; however, should you need a specialist for other medical concerns, neurologists, geriatric psychiatrists, and geriatricians all receive training in the evaluation and treatment of memory disorders.

If you're looking for a memory assessment clinic, contact your local Alzheimer's organization for a list of doctors, tests, and other helpful information.

In essence, my suggestion to you is to see if you can iron things out with your doctor first before switching. Remember, any type of change is difficult for an Alzheimer's patient. Ask for a moment alone with your physician so as to explain how you feel and what changes need to be made to best care for your patient. If your doctor is not willing to listen and consider your concerns, you have your answer! Find one that will.

"Pain unseen is worse than pain you can touch and feel."
Written by Memory People member Lisa Enderie Rado

Chapter 63

Hospitalization

A perfect example of what happens when Alzheimer's patients are taken out of their routine is when they are admitted into a hospital. Confusion will multiply about a thousandfold, and you will find yourself wondering what the heck just happened to them.

When my dad was in the hospital we couldn't convince him he was even *in* a hospital. New faces, strange surroundings, and beeping equipment only caused to overwhelm.

He was placed in a bed that was on the door side of the room while his roommate lay in the bed by the window. A curtain dividing the two beds gave my father almost a tunnel vision effect which made matters even worse. When people came to visit the other fellow, all my dad heard were several unfamiliar voices almost driving him mad.

He constantly insisted that someone needed to close doors on the other side of the room. But the problem was the "doors" didn't even exist. (And when I say constantly, I mean over and over.)

By the end of the second day his roommate was begging to be moved to another room. I asked him on the way out what had taken him so long. He told me, "I was trying to be polite, but I just can't take it anymore. I don't know how you do it."

After he was moved to another room, this left the bed by the window unoccupied. I asked the nurses if it was possible for my father to be moved by the door. I tried to explain that I believed my father would handle the situation so much better if he could see more of his surroundings. They stared at me as if I was insane. They had just had that bed made! Go figure.

At the time your patient is admitted you must insist that the hospital staff make a note in big bold letters in their medical chart that they are suffering from dementia. Tell the entire staff that your loved one is memory impaired.

Early the next morning I told his doctor that the nurses had refused to move Dad and explained my theory of why I felt it was important. To my surprise he said, "I'll be right back." Within the next hour my dad had a new view, now being able to look out the door and into the hall and out the window. It was like the difference between night and day.

My father was still in mass confusion, but by being able to see into the hallway he now had some sense that maybe he actually was in a hospital. Suddenly he was seeing patients pass by in wheelchairs and also hall walkers going by in their exposing hospital gowns.

I went outside to get some fresh air for a minute only to return to find a nurse standing over my dad with a clipboard, trying to get his prescription history out of him.

As soon as my father saw me he yelled, "Gary, will you tell this (well I won't use his exact words) that if she doesn't leave me alone I'm going to have her thrown out of my building and have her arrested."

There were too many new faces, too many people who didn't know how to handle someone with Alzheimer's, and too many professionals that wouldn't listen to the caregiver.

You can't just drop Alzheimer's patients off at the hospital and believe that they're going to be cared for. You need to be there physically and also be their voice. Every time my father went into the hospital, my sister and I would take shifts staying with him. The staff was going to have plenty of questions and the chance that they were going to receive the correct answer from him was very slim.

I just want you to be forewarned that a trip to the hospital only adds additional stress to the caregiver, and then when you finally get them home it could take days if not weeks for them to return to any kind of normalcy.

Stay by their side and be their advocate while they are there.

"I wanted a perfect ending. Now I've learned, the hard way, that some poems don't rhyme and some stories don't have a clear beginning, middle, and end.

Life is about not knowing, having to change, taking the moment and making the best of it without knowing what's going to happen next."

—Gilda Radner

Submitted by Memory People member June Newsome

Chapter 64

Don't Have a Caregiver Backup Plan? Make One!

Accidents happen. This well-known fact makes it imperative for the caregiver to devise a backup plan. This plan must be designed to have another person who can take over responsibilities in case of emergencies.

Let's say you trip over something and sprain or break your ankle. As you sit with your foot elevated, the Alzheimer's patient you're caring for will constantly ask, "What happened to your foot?"

You know how tiring it is to be asked over and over about your injuries. Well, now you will be asked twenty to thirty times a day, and that's probably an extremely low estimate.

So now you'll be hobbling around trying to care for the both of you. This is not a good scenario—trust me. I've been there.

It is the primary caregiver's responsibility to make sure

there's someone always ready, willing, and trained to step in when there's an emergency. I'm not just talking about broken bones here; there are doctors' appointments, medications, financial matters, etc. The list is long and you know it.

What happens if you die? Make certain ahead of time that the fate of your loved one will be placed in the right hands.

If you have power of attorney, papers need to be drawn up to have someone responsible enough to take charge should you not be there.

Do you really want the court to decide? No! I didn't think so. Unfortunately, if this actually happens, you won't be here. Decisions must be made now.

Meet with your attorney and have the appropriate papers drawn up. Explain the entire situation and that someone must be able to legally make the proper decisions in your absence.

Since the one you're caring for is unable to handle his or her own affairs, you must get busy immediately on this master plan.

You as the caregiver are of the utmost importance in the life of your loved one. Meet with your family members or friends and put a backup plan together. You never know when something could happen.

"Caregiving can take your heart places you never imagined, but despite its extraordinary challenges one rarely regrets the journey."

Written by Jack and Kim Linder.

Submitted by Memory People member Kim Linder, Host of the Caregiver Hour radio show.

Chapter 65

The Difference Between Alzheimer's and Dementia

Distinguishing between Alzheimer's and simple dementia is very hard for the average person. I have come to this conclusion from many conversations with confused caregivers everywhere.

In an article by Dr. Robert Stern, Director of the Boston University Alzheimer's Disease Center, Stern simply explained that "Dementia is a symptom, and Alzheimer's is the cause of the symptom. A good analogy to the term dementia is 'fever.' Fever refers to an elevated temperature, indicating that the person is sick, but it does not touch on any information on what is causing the sickness." What he's saying is that dementia is not the disease; it is one of the *symptoms* of the disease.

There are many causes of dementia, and some are reversible. But unfortunately, 70–80 percent of all cases occur from Alzheimer's, which is not reversible. In fact it is fatal!

Many old terms such as senility, having senior moments, or experiencing a second childhood have been replaced by the word "dementia." Dementia is not necessarily a normal part of aging, however. If it does present itself, the person showing signs should be checked out thoroughly. The significance of a correct diagnosis could make all the difference in putting the patient on the right track and possibly curing the problem.

Keeping in mind the differences between Alzheimer's and dementia, the most prominent one to look for is loss of memory, which leads into the decline of other cognitive skills such as language, attention span, decision making, and motor skills functions.

Fighting Alzheimer's includes educating the public to be aware of all the disabilities involved with the disease. This also means educating physicians. Over the past several years many doctors have seemed to become at ease with the inclination of diagnosing the patient with Alzheimer's a little too quickly when, in fact, it may be a form of dementia that could be reversible.

So remember this: when dealing with Alzheimer's or dementia, beginning with a proper diagnosis is essential so that the patient can immediately be prescribed the correct treatment or therapy and the family can plan ahead from this point, getting started on the right foot.

"Hope is a powerful emotion, but false hope can be devastating."
Written by Memory People member Gary Joseph LeBlanc

Chapter 66

Is Dementia Contagious?

Studies have shown that the stressful environment that is experienced by those caring for dementia patients brings on an elevated risk of depression, which can cause a form of dementia.

A fellow caregiver once asked me if I thought dementia was contagious. I responded, "Yes, in a manner of speaking, it seems you can start assuming the same symptoms of a loved one who is memory impaired."

Experts speculate that on average, caregivers of dementia patients provide care for a much longer period of time than other caregivers. This explains the high rate of depression.

Another cause of the symptoms of dementia is simply being overtired. I learned during the many years of caring for my dad that I could basically get by just napping, but this was not a healthy way to live. Getting a full night's sleep became virtually hopeless. I was constantly living on the edge of exhaustion.

This sort of caregiving is both physically and mentally overwhelming; in this lies the danger of developing depression. These demands can become more difficult with each passing day bringing along additional symptoms of stress such as: chronic anxiety, apathy, fatigue, frustration, and being short tempered. These in and of themselves can provide triggers for the onset of dementia.

It's one thing if you cannot keep track of your keys. This is most likely a sign that you're in desperate need of some respite. But if you can no longer remember what the keys are for, it may be time to have a discussion about the matter with your doctor.

Here are a few signs to be on the lookout for:

- Difficulty remembering things much more often than before
- Problems with learning new things
- Difficulty remembering how to do things you have done many times before
- Repeating yourself during the same conversation
- Trouble making decisions or handling money
- Unable to keep track of what has happened during a given day

Thankfully, dementia that develops from depression is reversible; this is why it's so important to discuss these fears with someone in the medical profession. Just the fact that you're worried about it should hopefully be enough to give you the courage to initiate the conversation.

Taking care of a person with dementia is an act of selfless love and an extremely important job. Make sure that you, as a caregiver, take care of your own well-being too. Don't be afraid to ask for help, especially toward the end of this undertaking. It becomes impossible to do it all alone.

"Let us be grateful to people who make us happy; they are the charming gardeners who make our soul blossom."

—Marcel Proust

Submitted by Memory People member Patrick Fisher

Chapter 67

Hospice: Accept All the Help That They Offer

If I could go back and change anything about how I cared for my dad, it would be that I put off accepting hospice care until very late in the disease. Now that I've had the chance to reflect back on those years, I definitely would have to answer, "I should have listened to my dad's doctor when he first suggested that I should get hospice involved."

Instead, I spent a long, lonely, and difficult year trying to do it all on my own, before finally opening my mind, and my door, to them. I had foolishly turned away the invaluable and much-needed help they offered to both of us.

I didn't doubt that hospice would approve him; Dad was definitely qualified. It was *I* that was holding back.

I had this notion that hospice basically meant immediate

death. I felt that by letting them into our lives I was giving up on my dad.

I understand now that hospice is designed to bring comfort to loved ones and their surrounding families.

Surprisingly, the very same afternoon I agreed to have Dad's doctor contact hospice, I received a call from the local hospice. By the next morning a social worker and a nurse were already at our house evaluating my dad. With all the proper paperwork filled out, he was approved the very next day.

The next thing I knew he was visited by his new hospice doctor. (I know, a doctor who actually makes house calls? I practically fainted!) Then his prescriptions started being delivered directly to our front door.

I wondered, "Could this get any better?" Well, it did. Before I knew it a home health aide was coming by to help bathe him two to three times a week. Also, his nurse/case manager came four–five days a week.

So to all of you caregivers who are at the end of your proverbial rope, please don't turn down any help that's available to you. Talk with your attending physician to see if he or she feels that your loved one is at the point where hospice should be involved.

I cannot stress how much help hospice was for us. I honestly doubt if I would have been able to keep my dad home "until his final breath" without their help, allowing him to, with comfort and with dignity, pass away in his own home.

Hospice is there to provide a high quality of comfort and also preserve the dignity of our loved ones' last days. They remove much of the stress so that caregivers are then able to concentrate on the important things, like saying goodbye.

The hospice workers became like family. Within ten minutes after my father's passing, they were on the phone helping make most of the arrangements. They handled so many of the things that I wouldn't have been able to wrap my mind around at that point.

Being overwhelmed with the sadness from the loss of my father and virtually going without sleep for the past month, they helped me with matters I couldn't even fathom.

Dear caregivers, listen closely—grab all the help you can get. There's no reason for you to go through this alone.

"Lord, with you to guide me I know that I will be strong."
Written by Memory People member Terri Newton Karam

Chapter 68

Choosing the Correct Adult Living Facility

A very difficult and challenging time in caregivers' lives will be when they decide it is time to research the possibility of an Adult Care Facility for their loved ones with Alzheimer's.

Making all the right choices is hard enough without the flood of guilt that surrounds it as well. This comes from caregivers feeling that they're actually giving up on taking responsibility for their patients; they know full well that the moment may soon come when they must endure the devastating pain of packing up their loved ones and their belongings and dropping them off somewhere.

I am often asked my opinion of the following scenario: "If loved ones fall on the floor and caregivers are not capable of picking them up, should they call 911? If so, is this a warning sign that they may no longer be able to give loved ones the quality of care they need?"

If this is you, step outside the box and be honest with yourself. Is it time to find full-time help outside the home?

Searching for an appropriate facility will be a time-consuming undertaking. It may be very difficult to single out the correct one, especially while carrying out your caregiver duties at the same time. I suggest that you talk to other caregivers at a local support group. You may get a feel for which facilities do or do not offer anything for patients suffering from the same disabilities.

Beware of glossy marketing brochures and "million-dollar tours." Don't put much stock in these as they can be far from accurate or truthful.

Instead, make a list of places to visit and show up unannounced. Using all of your senses, discern the quality that's actually provided.

If your loved one is suffering from Alzheimer's or other dementia-related symptoms, check for how qualified the staff is in dealing with the special needs that will come up in these cases.

For instance, ask how they deal with wandering patients. Even if your loved one has never wandered before, he or she may begin to, all of a sudden, because of the new environment.

Talk with the activity director to see what programs they have in-house for those who are memory impaired. Concern yourself with the quality of life they offer to their resident patients.

Another important matter is how they handle the late stages of the disease. Is the facility prepared for end stage Alzheimer's? Find out if patients will be able to continue to see their own physician. You will most likely have to drive yours to appointments yourself or pay extra for transportation.

Here are a few other tips:

Weigh your family member on the day he or she is admitted and closely monitor thereafter. Most facilities are only required to weigh their residents once a month. I have found that this allows for too big a window during which severe weight loss can occur. This usually leads to more serious health conditions, including malnutrition and dehydration.

Request a weekly weigh-in. Always talk to the nurse or dietary staff if you see five or more pounds have been lost.

Visit as often as possible, but do not establish a regular schedule. Vary your visits, being sure to be there during all shifts, both weekdays and weekends. Observe how their activities and mealtimes are conducted.

Bring a camera or video recorder to document any concerns that you may have with the way your loved one looks or how their environment appears.

Get to know the other providers who will be involved in the care of your loved one, especially CNAs, Home Health Aides, and physical and occupational therapy assistants. These people are the most hands-on and hardworking and will get to know your loved one intimately.

Further, make it a point to be present when the doctor or physician's assistant is on-site and speak with him or her directly about any concerns.

Ask questions, seek clarification, and note every conversation and request. Follow up diligently and hold management and staff accountable. If it comes down to it, even let them fear you.

Have a backup plan. Continue to visit other places and consider alternatives in the event that you might have to relocate your loved one. Granted, it will take time for adjustment, but do not ignore any red flags or obvious feelings of neglect on the part of your loved one.

Making these decisions is, without a doubt, among the most difficult for a caregiver because they have to be correct. If you have a sense that this time is coming upon you, be proactive.

Do your research ahead of time. The last thing you need is to be forced into making a rash decision.

"Grief is the most available untapped, emotional resource for personal transformation. We don't just get over our grief. Instead, we change our relationship to it."

—Unknown Author

Submitted by Memory People member Jennifer Swift-Kramer

Chapter 69

The Aftereffects of Caregiving

If you are a caregiver for a loved one who is slowly passing away from any disease, you will lose parts of your life that can take many years to recover, if ever.

Unfortunately, the chronic stress of caregiving isn't "over when it's over."

Certain side effects tend to linger on. For instance, forty-five percent of caregivers go through mild-to-severe depression for up to two to three years after their loved one has passed. Many never fully recover to once again enjoy a functional social life. A caregiver must learn to accept the changes one day at a time.

If this is you, it's highly unlikely that you will ever look at life in the same way again. You'll probably even neglect your own health care during and after the duties are over. I recall that in my case the last people I wanted to see were physicians or anyone else working in the medical profession. I had more than my fill of them, especially throughout the last six months of my father's life. I think it was about a year after Dad's passing before I could bear to see a doctor for any reason.

Then there is the problem of finances. Facts show that one-third of caregivers report their income to be in the poverty level to near-poverty level range. According to a high percentage of caregivers that I have heard from, the reason is that they found it necessary to quit their jobs. After their loved one dies they resurface in the current world of high unemployment. These people are trying to steady themselves and finally get back on their feet, while at the same time living in a world of dismay. It's hard to describe exactly how it feels, but I can tell you it's like living in a world of emptiness.

For almost a decade I was devoted to the cause of caring for my dad. But when that period ended, all of a sudden it was like a floodgate was opened. It wasn't like a gentle stream flowing by; it was more like shooting the white water rapids of newly released freedom! For years prior I could barely get out to go to the grocery store, and suddenly I could go wherever I wanted, whenever I wanted. But the truth of the matter was, I really didn't feel like going anywhere at all. For years I promised myself an overdue vacation, maybe visit some old friends. Heck, I couldn't even get myself to leave the county!

What I did was to find myself looking for something or someone else to take care of. Anybody! For instance, a sick friend with the flu, a dying plant, or if the cat sneezed I was ready to rush over and hand her a tissue . . . it didn't matter. What finally happened was that I found deep fulfillment in the helping of other caregivers.

If you know any caregivers, or you are one yourself, be aware that, after the loss, there is a recovery period to walk through. Caregivers are notorious for saying everything is fine when, in reality, it is far from it. Let's give each other a call; that's what good friends do: help each other in times of need.

"I learned that courage was not the absence of fear, but the triumph over it. The brave man is not he who does not feel afraid, but he who conquers that fear."

—Nelson Mandela

Submitted by Memory People member Bernadette Brady

Chapter 70

Veteran's Administration's REACH Program

It seems that major budget cuts headline the news every week. Despite this, the Veteran's Administration (VA) has begun implementing a caregiver support program that is becoming available nationwide.

Finally, there is a department of our government that has acknowledged that it makes perfectly good sense, morally and fiscally, to invest in the caregivers of our beloved veterans. These American heroes are best served when provided with the mental and physical tools with which to live their lives as independently as possible, for as long as possible, surrounded by devoted family members and friends. A key means to this end is through the education and support of their dedicated caregivers.

Another available option is, of course, institutionalization; however, the cost can be as high as $70,000.00 per year, per patient. Making a move this life changing may be able to be avoided now, with the creation of this new and valuable educational program. Whether our veterans are hospitalized or living outside of their homes, the VA will be lending caregiver support.

Fifty-four million adults in the United States provide care to an adult family member or friend and are not compensated. Forty percent say they didn't have a choice in taking on their caregiver role, and more than 50 percent have experienced medium to high levels of stress as a result of the demands laid upon them.

The new program is aptly titled "REACH" which is an acronym for "Resources for Enhancing Alzheimer's Caregivers' Health." Although the project is still fairly new, it has already proven to provide stress-reducing solutions, at the same time furnishing vital resources along with training. It also focuses on personal health. This can give much-needed help to caregivers as they struggle to assist their beloved veterans.

REACH has been instrumental in providing caregivers with the following: twelve individual home and telephone counseling sessions, a Caregiver Quick Guide with forty-eight behavioral and stress topics, education on safety and patient behavior management along with direction for their own health and well-being. As a result, reports have come in that burdens seem reduced, and a noticeable drop in symptoms of depression has occurred.

Dr. Linda Nichols is with the VA Medical Center in Memphis, Tennessee, and also coauthor of a study on the REACH program. She said, "The intervention provided time for themselves, which caregivers never have enough of. It also improved our caregivers' knowledge to manage care, made them feel more confident and competent as they formed bonds with the VA staff supporting them, and decreased the inevitable feelings of isolation and loneliness that comes from a selfless but very sacrificial duty of care."

I believe that since there is no cure for Alzheimer's, educating ourselves is our best defense.

The VA is rolling out REACH on a national basis through home-based primary care. Because of this, caregivers of veterans diagnosed with disabilities besides Alzheimer's, such as spinal cord injuries and traumatic brain injuries, will also receive much-needed assistance.

REACH is the first national clinical exercise in proven behavioral intervention for dementia caregivers. There are local caregiver support coordinators available to assist veterans of all eras, along with their caregivers, in applying and understanding VA's caregiver benefits.

The VA has opened a toll-free National Caregiver Support Line, serving as a primary resource/referral center, to aid veterans or others seeking this information. Calls will be taken Monday through Friday 8:00 a.m. to 11:00 p.m. and Saturday 10:30 a.m. to 6:00 p.m. Eastern time. The toll-free number is (855) 260-3274. I also encourage you to visit the VA's caregiver website: <u>www.caregiver.va.gov</u>

"Where is it at when you say you want to go home? If I could only take you there, I would!"

Written by Memory People member Kathie Byars

Chapter 71

Long-Term Care Insurance

Long-Term Care Insurance is growing in popularity here in the United States. However, premiums have risen drastically in recent years. The costs of coverage can be quite expensive, especially if an applicant waits until retirement age to purchase it.

It has become common knowledge that people are living longer and using more benefits these days.

In most states, regulators must approve rate hikes. Even so, most policies are running into the thousands of dollars per year.

This insurance could help protect your lifetime savings against the cost of nursing facilities and professional home health care. Without it you may ultimately drain all of your assets until you finally qualify for Medicaid.

If you should decide to look into purchasing a policy, here are a few things to keep in mind:

First, find a broker who specializes in the field of long term care. Be sure this person understands all the essentials. There are a lot of details to go over and many different coverages to choose from.

Next, compare prices. You may pay thousands of dollars more than necessary if you should go with the wrong company.

Finally, plan ahead. It is best if you buy your policy before you reach the age of sixty, after which, policies are automatically priced higher.

Long-Term Care Insurance can be complicated. Be sure to research it thoroughly. Listen carefully to the broker and ask questions about anything you're not sure about. You're planning for your future!

Your premiums may or may not be eligible for income tax deductions. Most tax qualified policies require that you pay for the first ninety days of your care yourself. You need to be careful, though, as the accrued costs during those ninety days may exceed the amount of money you will save in tax deductions. If you're up there in age, you may want to take this into consideration.

Experts recommend that the cost of your premium does not surpass 7 percent of your annual income. With the price of this insurance, this may be difficult.

I truly wish everyone could afford this insurance. There's no better feeling than to assure your independence and to not have to rely on others. This is one way to plan ahead for your senior years or in case you develop any disabilities, such as Alzheimer's.

My biggest concern, however, is that many people will be unable to afford this insurance in today's economy.

"Some people come into our lives and quickly go. Some people move our souls to dance. They awaken us to a new understanding with the passing whisper of their wisdom. Some people make the sky more beautiful to gaze upon. They stay in our lives for awhile, leave footprints on our hearts, and we are never, ever the same."

—Flavia Weedn

Submitted by Memory People member D. Victor Pellegrino

Chapter 72

After the Loss

I find it very difficult to adequately express the depth of feeling that permeated my soul after losing my father. I'm not sure if I will ever get over the loss; I guess I'm just hoping to get used to it.

For days, weeks, and even months afterward, I experienced a myriad of emotions: sadness, fear, shock, confusion, anger, guilt, exhaustion, a sense of being cheated, and even an unpleasant emptiness. Even now, when I feel as if I am moving on, a wave of overwhelming sorrow swells up inside of me. Having cared for my father for so many years, it felt as if my body had almost gone into shock when I fully realized that all my responsibilities had been lifted.

In the days immediately following his passing I was completely occupied in making final arrangements. These tasks were mentally difficult, but it felt as if I was still just carrying out my caregiving duties. Then it was like a switch had suddenly been turned off. I got so used to Hospice constantly coming and going, always having some presence in the house, when all of a sudden—BAM! I was all by myself. The only way I can describe it is that I felt hollow, as if I was living in a void.

The summer Dad died, in an attempt to change my state of mind, I decided to remodel the inside of my home. I chose bright and bold colors. I needed to put some life back into the house in order to keep my mind from wandering and grieving. Although the work took me weeks longer than I had first estimated, just keeping busy proved to be very therapeutic.

Everyone grieves differently. My sister, for instance, built a beautiful memorial garden in her backyard. Myself, I write, although the first couple of weeks I wasn't ready to put anything down on paper. Once I resumed writing it was as if I finally exhaled.

If the painful yearning for your loved one doesn't seem to begin dissolving with time, it might be helpful to seek out a support group. There is something comforting about sharing your feelings with a group of people who have suffered a similar tragedy.

When grieving the loss of someone close, take care that the depression doesn't lead into something worse, such as thoughts of suicide. Should this happen, it's imperative that the griever seek out someone to talk with. Just speaking of your pain and hopelessness can relieve a tremendous sense of pressure.

Give yourself time. The yearning for a loved one can be stronger than the depression itself. Once that person is gone, you will miss them, even hunger for them. We don't completely realize how much the presence of a loved one is desired until that person is taken away.

Don't underestimate the power of grief. It is one of man's strongest emotions.

Author's Conclusion

Throughout the journey of writing this book for Rick Phelps, I've learned to admire this man's courage in being so open and transparent about his life. His willingness to discuss his disabilities to help others shows what a selfless man he truly is.

I have acquired so much pristine knowledge from working on this project. I only wish I could have used this information during the ten-year campaign of caring for my own beloved father. I believe that this new perception would have made me a better caregiver.

I honestly feel that, between this book and my previous one, Staying Afloat in a Sea of Forgetfulness, *we have made great strides in providing invaluable and significant resources in bestowing quality care for the memory impaired.*

I would like to give endless thanks to all the "Memory People" members who donated their poems and quotes, helping to keep this book on the lighter side of a very dark subject.

I also need to give a shout-out to Holly Beth Michaels who helped me immensely in editing and making this book what it is.

Lately, I have watched how the world has moved forward in

fighting against Alzheimer's and dementia. It has truly touched my soul, but then there are times when I'm out at a grocery store for example, waiting in the checkout line, having a conversation with the person next to me, and I realize that they truly have no understanding of the excessive hardships of those suffering from these diseases and what their families are enduring.

This tells me we still have a lot of work to do. Collectively, we can help spread the much-needed awareness to the general public. I believe someday we will defeat this dreadful disease, which would in turn allow people to enjoy their "Golden Years" the way they were meant to.

Thank you everyone.

Sincerely,
Gary Joseph LeBlanc

Index

CPSIA information can be obtained at www.ICGtesting.com
Printed in the USA
LVOW040007230712

291113LV00002B/1/P